WINNING RUNNING

SUCCESSFUL 800M & 1500M RACING AND TRAINING

BY PETER COE

THE CROWOOD PRESS

First published in 1996 by
The Crowood Press Ltd
Ramsbury, Marlborough
Wiltshire SN8 2HR

British Library Cataloguing-in-Publication Data

A catalogue record for this book is available from the British Library

ISBN 1 85223 997 2

Table 1 (Table 4.2 pp192), Table 6 (Table 3.8 pp144), Table 4 (Table 3.5 pp137),
Fig 7, (Fig 3.10 pp161), Fig 8 (Fig 3.11 pp162), Fig 9 (adapted from Fig 3.11 pp162),
Fig 10 (Fig 3.12 pp163), Fig 11 (Fig 3.9pp160)
From: *Training Distance Runners* by D.E. Martin and P.N. Coe, Champaign,
IL: Leisure Press. Copyright 1991 by David E. Martin and Peter N. Coe.
Reprinted by permission of Human Kinetics Publishers. Figures in brackets
refer to references in *Training Distance Runners.*

All photographs from author collection, by photographers Mark Shearman
(p 57–8, 112), Peter Tempest (p96), VG Foto (p102), Dolf Preisig (p108), Beat Marti (p47),
Daily Mirror (p119) and Sheffield Newspapers (p62).

Printed and bound by J. W. Arrowsmith Ltd, Bristol

CONTENTS

FOREWORD

Over the years many books have been written about middle distance running. But this book is different. How can the father who coached his son to thirteen world records not be able, better than others, to distil sound advice that will illuminate the many problems of health, diet, psychology, fatigue and race tactics for coaches and runners everywhere?

Sebastian Coe's great career spanned nearly twenty years. He dominated running in the late 1970s and 1980s, and helped to restore to British running the respect of the rest of the world.

This book, with a wealth of practical detail, using reason not dogmatism, explains clearly how athletes may generate in themselves the will to win. It roundly condemns drug abuse and cheating and relies on developing self-knowledge to achieve as nearly as possible the athlete's full potential. The subject is endlessly fascinating and this excellent book will surely find a happy place on the shelves of athletes and coaches up and down Britain and around the world. I wish it all success.

Sir Roger Bannister

ACKNOWLEDGEMENTS

I am indebted to Dr J. Humphreys of Leeds and Dr C. Williams of Loughborough – two physiologists from whom I learned so much. It was through their knowledge that I was able to confirm scientifically the ideas I had formed in the beginning.

The basic physiology of the training zones is sound: I have learned from, and owe a lot to, my old friend and colleague Dr David E. Martin. He is Professor of Physiology at Georgia State University, and a consultant to TAC/USA. He runs a human performance laboratory.

Occasionally one or two other coaches were able to make their own special contribution. The first was Gordon Surtees, by two separate and wise observations early in my coaching career. Next came the drive and enthusiasm of the British Milers Club, together with the right races it provided. Before Seb Coe went to Loughborough University I asked George Gandy to set up and supervise a complete circuit and strength training regime with the aim being to improve 400m speed. This he did very well throughout Seb's years there.

Good long-term planning and a sound structure are essential to any enterprise, as is the availability of adequate funding. As chief national coach Frank Dick had a difficult role to play. Regardless of the outcome or the reasons for it, what he attempted to achieve would have left the coaching side of our sport on a sounder and more advanced base.

In a long time in athletics Sir Arthur Gold has made his indelible mark, for honesty and fair play.

From the beginning, club and school competition, particularly in the early days with tough cross-country running in Sheffield, helped to forge character and the will to win.

Later, and especially in 1983 and during the 1984 pre-Olympic build-up, it was the loyalty and the help in training by the members of Haringey A.C. that contributed greatly to the tremendously successful Olympic outcome. The success of this help was due in no small part to the drive and enthusiasm of John Hovell, a great motivator of the participating athletes. In that Olympics year it was the help and support of coach Joe Newton of York High Shool, Illinois and his family during Seb's acclimatising spell in the US prior to arriving in Los Angeles that deserves my gratitude.

Then there are the media, among whom I admit I have my favourites and some long-lasting friends, but even when occasionally not exactly sympathetic they acted as a powerful spur and certainly helped to keep the public interested in what we did. My records and race analyses would be very incomplete without the kind general assistance and video help of the BBC and ITV.

Not least are the race promoters. All meetings, great and small, need organizing, none more so than the big permit meetings. These are the great shop windows of our sport and its champions and the big promoters carry heavy burdens. The behind-the-scenes build-up to a big grand prix meeting is an exercise in international logistics. All the meetings depend on an army of true amateurs, that loyal band without whom meetings simply could not take place. They should never be forgotten and what should always be remembered is that they are people like any others, just trying to do their best. Many of them will have been in the sport longer than most of the competitors.

Finally, as I have touched on records and race analyses, I must reserve a special mention for the 'master chroniclers' – the statisticians. Authors find them handy as well!

INTRODUCTION

The aim of this book is to provide the basis for producing winners. It is to get coaches and athletes to think, and think big – to go for gold, and to work with enthusiasm and conviction to be the best.

The book is dedicated to Seb Coe, the outstanding runner of his time. He enjoyed the enormous success that came from winning Olympic gold and silver medals and setting many world records, and he bore the attendant pressures of his worldwide fame with civility and dignity.

Throughout the continual increase of these pressures, in no small part created by the exceptional length of his career at the top, he never allowed himself to be diverted from the single-minded pursuit of our unattainable goal of complete perfection.

Despite the cruelty of arbitrary authority and the illnesses to which very highly trained athletes are prone, his belief in his own ability never wavered and it has been carried over into his new professional life off the track. I cannot believe that any coach has been so well rewarded, not only by his athlete's success but with such faith and trust in his efforts as I have received.

Seb Coe became an all-time great in the history of athletics. The conditioning and training content of this book accurately describe many of the methods I used in his coaching, but presented in a form usable by adequately trained runners. But it is much more than that. This book also stems from his unique, single-minded dedication to the pursuit of his chosen excellence and his willingness to make the many sacrifices necessary for its achievement. Not least, it is a testament to the great synergistic power of a truly trusting relationship between a coach and an athlete.

The examples of the training sessions used are specific to competing successfully at 800m and 1500m but this should not obscure the main thrust of this book, which is about winning. The fundamental principles and attitudes expressed are relevant to all competitive running.

Because world-class times in 800m and 1500m races are such difficult targets, it is vital that coaches and athletes have a thorough grasp of all the constituent elements of these events.

This book provides an in-depth analysis of the 800m and 1500m races. A carefully detailed breakdown is necessary for understanding what is required to race and win and to appreciate just how heavy are the demands on coach and athlete of middle distance training for gold medal performances. Without such an analysis it is easy to overlook small but important details. A systematic examination of all these details in their right sequence provides a sound guide to the construction of a correct training plan.

I have not given any examples of workouts or training schedules of well-known athletes. Despite similarities athletes are always individuals, so schedules not tailored to individual readers can be very misleading and are unlikely to be sound guides to constructing ideal personal training programmes.

The correct training can only be derived from a careful analysis of the events, coupled with continuous assessment of the athlete. This book emphasises developing this analytical approach just as much to the art as the science of training winners. The training described in this book is not a simple recipe or formula for guaranteed success, it is a statement of the basic principles for building lasting success in these middle distance events.

There is so much to learn about middle distance racing that any one section of this book cannot completely cover it's subject, but there is enough in each to be a guide to any further reading and study the reader might want to pursue. If in describing this approach to training and racing there seems to be any repetition or over-emphasis it is only because of the importance of the points being made.

I have dwelt much on motivation in training and competition and what it takes to be a consistent winner at the highest level. I have had the privilege and the pleasure of spending many long years as an active partner in the pursuit of ath-

letic excellence. I have never wavered in my belief that winning is the name of the game and the price of the unremitting effort is well worth it. As a coach my only aim is to enable the athlete to achieve superlative and definitive performances.

There are times when it is necessary to take racing risks with an athlete still learning the trade. Inevitably, despite some heroic efforts, it will sometimes result in losing, but the knowledge that can be gained from these defeats is priceless. Defeat is always defeat, but it is also an opportunity to find out what might be going wrong. Our county championships are a wasteland of neglected opportunities to experiment by our would-be high flyers.

Experimenting, and choosing the right moments for it, is essential to progress but I believe that very few athletes are prepared to go beyond what they perceive to be their limits to discover whether the impossible might just be possible – especially when youth is on their side.

Seb and I were still experimenting when he was a hardened and senior athlete. Once, when it was early in the year for us and at a semi-major meeting, defeat was only just averted when it appeared that we had got our sums wrong. All round there was dire and ill-informed comment. It seemed that only a couple of people understood what had been done; they were two long standing observers of the domestic and international scene – Stan Greenberg and Mel Watman.

Over the years nothing has arisen to cause me to change the methods or the principles on which my coaching is based, but there are two important areas to which I came to give even more care and emphasis. One is ensuring that training sessions are hard enough to increase mental toughness. This enhances the will to handle future training and competition, thus building justifiable confidence.

The other is maintaining strength training later into the season to preserve racing strength closer to peaking. Mature athletes who are well into their careers, but can still just handle the very hard sessions necessary for continued success, need progressively more time between the tough sessions to permit proper recovery.

Along the way there are ample opportunities to watch other competitors and observe the difference between winners and losers, between those who simply get lucky once or twice and those who stay at the top for long and successful careers. One or two good seasons is not success; ten years at the top is. Studying the opposition can be very useful – they reveal a lot by what they say and do off the track.

While this book is about training, much of which is very demanding, it would be incomplete without some reference to behaviour and motivation in an effort to present a fuller picture of training and racing to win – after all, the body does have a head.

Unfortunately, for serious runners, especially the elite athlete, much of what is written on sports psychology is concerned with team games, and mainly inapplicable to those in the highly individual sport of competitive running.

For the runner an Olympic stadium packed with tens of thousands of people is a very lonely place indeed. The athlete is without any team support, without team members to provide an excuse for a poor performance, and all the rest of the field are enemies. Only the development of a steely self-reliance and confidence can see one through these moments successfully. It takes years of hard experience to prepare for such intense pressure but where and when possible, and the earlier the better, some good advice from those who have experienced this pressure and who were both thinking and successful can be very helpful. Seb believes that had he made the 1976 Olympics, if only to experience that kind of pressure, it would have ensured him a better performance in the 1980 Moscow 800m.

There are those who, for doctrinaire reasons unconnected with sport, are trying hard to make the facts fit their theories and would deny our youth any competition. At best they grudgingly permit only mild participation. Fortunately, mankind is naturally a very competitive animal and there will always be those who seek success and try to be better than the rest.

In every sphere of human activity people are trying to extend their knowledge and experience of what is possible. Times will improve, records will fall, and like it or not, someone, somewhere in the world, is striving body and soul to be the best at whatever they do. If environment has an important role in human development then try to create one that enhances progress, not hinders it. We all have the power to make some modification to our environment.

I hope that this book will help coaches and athletes who are serious about winning, especially those who desire to be the best. Yes, it is a long, hard road. Anything that is worthwhile does not come easily, but there is a tremendous high in being the best – or as a coach, just having had a part in it.

I have found my coaching and the philosophy on which it is based to be consistently true during the long haul to the top and because, for a long time, I have suc-cessfully practised what I preach, this book is more than just an opinion. It is what I know and what has worked to pro-duce Olympic gold medals and world records. The desire to be the best is my strongest message. You must thoroughly understand what it is you are trying to achieve, think first, but think big and then go for gold.

≡1≡
HEALTH

In the pursuit of physical excellence there is no greater asset than good health. It is the foundation for the consistency needed for successful training. The *Collins English Dictionary* defines health as 'the state of being bodily and mentally vigorous and free from disease.' This is a good definition with no need to include freedom from injury, when the intention is to stay vigorous. However, it is much more difficult for an ambitious runner in hard training to meet this ideal state whereas it is far easier to maintain for the ordinary sportsman or woman.

This is so because success at the top demands a very high level of specific fitness. The very hard training and the great stress applied to produce the necessary adaptation are so intense that they render athletes more prone to infections and overuse injuries than less ambitious runners. The body cells of highly trained athletes seem to be more permeable to invaders than those of runners training at lower intensities.

Because the demands at the top level are so severe it is vital that every training session is well thought out, specific and does not involve any unnecessary work. There is neither time and energy to waste nor any safe margin of health; the top men and women are always working close to the limit of staying healthy.

The care to avoid excessive stress even precludes the use of many other sports for fun and relaxation. While a little table tennis or refreshing swimming is fine, a tough session of hard court tennis is risky, while indulging in rugby or soccer, supposing there is energy left over from training, is sheer folly even in the strongly recommended end of season lay-off. A professional soccer player can take a fairly hard knock and with a little treatment can return to his sport after a few days. But the constant repetitive work required in distance training can soon turn even the slightest injury into a serious impediment to an athlete's training.

Effective training is the means whereby one becomes able, or more able, to perform a task. It requires good planning by coach and athlete. Taking short cuts involves departing from the plan and this seriously reduces the value of the work. By adhering to the plan the athlete becomes fitter and more disciplined. As the body and mind are improved simultaneously an important lesson is learned: long-term goals can be achieved

15

only by dedication and hard work, which, with appropriate recoveries, produce that very important element of training – consistency. Without it there is no lasting progress.

Fitness is measured as the level of adaptation to your lifestyle. This includes all other activities besides athletic training. Adopting a healthier lifestyle is a major improvement in itself and the athlete then has a greater resistance to all the other stresses of life; being ill and unfit to train is a loss of consistency. To look back on a long period of consistent work gives an athlete a high level of confidence in training, which is essential for successful competition.

BASIC GUIDE TO DIET

A few words on diet are fitting, because deficiencies in the diet can affect health, more so that of athletes in hard training. There are plenty of reference books giving excellent advice on diet, so these few simple guidelines should suffice.

Eat a balanced diet based on the following proportions: protein 15 per cent, fat 20 to 25 per cent, carbohydrates 60 to 65 per cent. If the diet contains enough red meat (or other sources of easily assimilated iron), pasta, a variety of fresh or lightly cooked vegetables and some fresh fruit – the whole yielding enough calories to maintain your best competition weight – it is unlikely that you will have to spend money on expensive supplements. If you do, buy a multi-vitamin type because the drug companies and manufacturers have spent a lot of time and effort getting the correct balance.

Note that multivitamin supplements are not the same as megavitamin supplements, which are a waste of money. The daily needs for all vitamins and trace elements are met with very small amounts. Any excess water-soluble vitamins will only make expensive urine, and excess fat-soluble compounds will be stored, possibly with serious side-effects as is true of heavy doses of an iron supplement.

It is unlikely that a sensible diet will fail to provide an adequate supply of vitamins and essential trace elements. The following are found in several different breakfast cereals, each supplying between 25 and 50 per cent of the recommended daily allowance in a 30g serving: niacin, iron, vitamins B1, B2, B6 and B12, folic acid, vitamin D, calcium, magnesium and zinc.

Careful blood monitoring will indicate any iron deficiency (not just anaemia). The full blood profiling of an athlete training at a high level requires an extensive printout as there are many markers to be checked that might reveal a variety of impending problems. Should there be any concern about iron levels any good sports dietitian or a book on diet will list the foods that inhibit iron absorption – but be safe and take good medical advice.

Do not worry obsessively over every mouthful; diet deficiencies do not develop overnight. Common sense should preclude continually stuffing away fried and fatty convenience foods. In being fit, simply take pleasure in what you eat, do not eat just for pleasure. Finally, alas, alcohol has no good role in the diet.

PRE-COMPETITION MEALS

There is not any need to eat food close to a race, in fact it should be avoided. During the warm-up and with the effect of pre-race tension there is a pronounced shift of blood away from the digestive system. Any significant quantity of food still in the stomach can cause distress. To ensure that this does not happen avoid the intake of any fatty food during the last pre-race meal. Fat is much less easily digested than carbohydrates.

Other than the individual's own taste there is no need for liquid intake for short duration races – some runners take great care to avoid the feeling of any liquid at all slopping around in their stomachs before and during a race. In a very hot climate it is necessary to avoid dehydration, but staying in the shade will reduce the temptation to drink too much liquid.

A RELEVANT LIFESTYLE

Over-training occurs when the total load on the athlete exceeds the resistance of both body and mind to the applied stress. The total load consists of the whole lifestyle and not just the training. The resulting condition, unless quickly relieved, will soon usher in physical and mental fatigue. The initial symptoms might be only lassitude or poor performance but the athlete can soon become vulnerable to bacterial and viral infections and even to serious physical damage.

Always take a rest day every seventh day, or as close to it as possible, and at the end of the racing season take a full month off from training and maintain only your flexibility routine. This will allow your body to repair the hidden microtraumas that the tissues incur and lose any aches and pains resulting from the very hard physical work. Substituting long, hard games of tennis or soccer during this lay-off will have a negative effect on your end of season recovery. Playing these games incurs an unnecessary risk of injury.

Athletes who are keen to start cross-country or road racing as soon as their principal season ends should be asked what they really want from running. Is it to be just a good all-rounder or is it to select an event in which to be a top performer and a winner when it really matters?

STRESS

Figure 1 shows the many factors contributing to the total stress on an athlete.

a) In mechanics, $STRESS = \dfrac{LOAD}{UNIT\ AREA}$

b) In simpler training terms this can be written as
$$\dfrac{LIFESTYLE}{ATHLETE} \quad \text{and} \quad X\,100 = \%\,LOAD$$

c)
(Lifestyle)
Training ± Study/Work ± Finance ± Domestic/Family ± Expectations/Pressures ± Relaxation ± Sleep ± Coach Relationship ± Confidence ± Eagerness - Lethargy ± Sex ± General Peer Pressures

$$TOTAL\ STRESS = \dfrac{\rule{3cm}{0.4pt}}{YOU}$$

Fig 1   An equation representing stress.

It is not possible to give each item a numerical value, but the diagram illustrates the complexity of the whole problem and what constitutes excess. The individual factors comprising the load are shown as being positive or negative. Whether they are in excess or insufficient they will all affect the load, while some like lethargy or peer pressure are best minimized. Clearly all these factors need to be carefully balanced to permit the amount of training required to achieve the planned objective.

To illustrate the point of maintaining good health and consistency when in training, a theoretically numerical load (as in line b) should mainly be a little less than 100 per cent, but when building up to a major peak there will always be some short periods, perhaps two or three days, when the loading may be more. This will certainly occur when attempting supercompensation. During recovery periods the load should be as little as possible.

It requires only a brief look at lifestyle in line C to recognize the need for a careful self-assessment and how important mental discipline is to your life and a successful athletic career.

WARMING UP AND COOLING DOWN

Develop a suitable warm-up before training and racing, as it helps to prevent injury. Many middle distance runners waste energy doing excessive warm-ups, particularly before races. A suitable warm-up means doing only enough to do the job properly, and not any more. This must include a thorough stretching routine. This should be started only after the warm-up has commenced – stretching should never be done when cold. After stretching, the warm-up can be resumed at a slightly faster pace until the athlete is warm enough to perform safely those few fast strides that complete the session. The warm-up will probably include a fairly fast burst of running for about 300m, but the athlete should conserve energy by finding the shortest complete warm-up.

A good and careful cool-down should follow immediately after any training session or race. Sometimes, after big races, the pressure of the organizers and the media makes this difficult. Do not be rude – be tough but imaginative. Here I admit to a dilemma because, in the main, I do not like victory laps. They belong only to the winner and only if the winning performance merits one: and never to whoever comes second. The dilemma stems from the fact that the best cool-down after a very hard race would be to continue on past the tape and run another lap or two at a brisk steady pace. If this is inappropriate the best solution would be to finish the run-off first, on the inside grass, and do all the talking later.

The first few minutes of the cool-down run should be at a brisker pace than the rest, because maintaining a copious flow of oxygen-rich blood to the muscles reduces the risk of stiffness by ridding the tissue of unwanted metabolites. The remainder of the cool-down is only a steady jog to ensure that the flushing-out process is completed.

INJURY

In the unfortunate event of traumatic injury do nothing more than orthodox first aid unless you are expert in the correct procedures. Even something you might think simple and obvious to do might be very unwise. Get expert assistance urgently.

There are two main risks and types of injury. Sprinters, jumpers and those doing specific speed training face risks like sudden muscle pulls and tendon strains. Those doing serious distance work are more likely to incur over-use injuries. Teenagers have an increased risk of lower limb stress fractures, often to the lower third of the tibia.

No one should submit the lower limbs to the undue stress of running across the side of slopes. Run only straight up or down them. Do not continually run in the road with the same leg close to the kerb, as this has the same effect as having one leg shorter than the other. Both these activities frequently produce stress fractures or injury caused through imbalance.

THE TRAINING REGIME

Ensure that the training regime neither exceeds nor continually hovers too near the athlete's limit, which is different for each individual. A well balanced diet, a comprehensive flexibility programme and regular orthopaedic, osteopathic, biomechanical and physiological checks will greatly lessen the risk of injury. If orthotics are needed, be sure to have some for everyday walking and standing around, some for distance work and some for racing shoes – each pair will be different.

If, to avoid or overcome staleness, more relaxed amusement and less training is indicated, it is very counter-productive to become frenetic and extreme in play. Dedication to the training regime needed to reach the top cannot always be fun or produce a barrel of laughs. Nothing should be allowed to impair eating regular, balanced meals and having a regular, sound eight hours sleep, best commenced well before midnight.

The intense training routine undertaken by those going for gold constitutes a special kind of health risk, quite different from the normal risks of the less active. Therefore it needs a higher level of continual monitoring, but be calm and rational; becoming obsessively worried is neurotic and bad for your health. It is very unlikely that a hypochondriac will achieve a high level of performance.

Fit to Train

There is little information on preventive medicine for athletes outside specialist physiology and sports medicine journals. Likewise, there is not enough awareness of the need to monitor thoroughly the condition of athletes who are in hard training and are competing seriously, so the following needs stressing.

Coaching is managing, and good management is good planning, so plan well ahead for success. This includes building up your health team in advance. Seek out readily available medical backups before you need them, and find a GP who is sympathetic to athletes.

When evaluating fitness for training before and during a hard regime, regular health checks are necessary. Comprehensive blood monitoring – when carefully explained – can give advance warning of a breakdown in health. Merely knowing that an athlete's haemoglobin level is not abnormal is not enough.

Runners on high training distances are especially prone to iron depletion. There are various reasons for this iron loss but the major contributor is the haemolysis (destruction of red blood cells) caused by the continual hard impact of the feet, mainly the heels, with the ground. Some of the iron lost by the break up of the red blood cells and other causes is recovered by haptoglobin so that haptoglobin and ferritin (the primary iron storage molecule) are good markers for the body's level of iron stores.

Iron depletion is not iron deficiency or anaemia. Haemoglobin levels might be in the normal range while leaving the body short of iron for other purposes such as the iron-containing enzymes. Diagnosis and any ongoing iron supplementation should be under medical control.

An electrocardiogram (ECG) should be taken under exercise conditions. Some abnormalities only show under stress, and the resting ECGs of some athletes might show an irregularity that is quite harmless.

When mechanical faults start to develop, the body, by its remarkable ability to compensate, tends to hide them. In a sedentary lifestyle this might not matter for a long time but when in continuous hard training an uncorrected fault can turn very quickly into injury. If not correctly and promptly diagnosed and treated it is only a short step from the acute to the chronic. Prevention, being so much better than cure, is the best reason for consulting a good biomechanics clinic for regular monitoring. Such a clinic will have a video playback facility and computer graphics, which are invaluable for analysing movement.

For example, when these are used for gait analysis a whole chain of related faults is often uncovered, which otherwise might not be seen. Examining a poor footplant can often reveal structural faults in the skeleton. A spine or pelvis that has become misaligned can, among other things, give the effect of running with one leg shorter than the other. If detected early enough these faults are soon corrected by a qualified osteopath.

A word on general health. Coaches who are tuned in to their athletes are soon aware of any altered mood states. While problems of this nature have to be addressed and advice given where appropriate, they may arise in areas that the coach is not trained to handle and may require specialist advice. It is one thing to be a trusted friend and guide, but quite another to allow yourself to become so bogged down with social problems that you cannot effectively pursue your principal objective.

Consideration of the physiological, biomechanical and mental aspects of training underlines the necessity of regular total monitoring.

≡2≡
STRENGTH AND FITNESS TESTS

DIAGNOSTIC TESTS

There are runners who seem to be performing quite well but are often, quite unknown to themselves, not reaching their full potential because of a lack of specific or all-round strength. The following simple tests are worth trying, by beginners and experienced runners, because they might reveal gaps in their total conditioning. Until an athlete discovers his or her strengths and weaknesses, specific training or exercises to enhance or remedy them cannot be planned.

The following tests give a good guide to general physical fitness.

Balke Test

The athlete covers as much distance as possible in 15 minutes. The oxygen intake can be estimated from this distance. Divide the distance run (in metres) by 15 to give the speed in metres per minute.

From this speed subtract 133, multiply by 0.172, then add 34.4 to give the oxygen intake in ml/kg/min.

Standing Broad Jump

A standing jump of the athlete's height plus less than 10 per cent is weak. A jump of the athlete's height plus 25 per cent or more is strong.

Hopping Test

Mark off an accurate 25m. On one leg only, hop the full distance. A good 800m male runner will cover this distance in 10 hops, a good female in 11. Repeat using the other leg and compare the relative strengths.

50m Dash

A time of slower than 6.5 seconds is a sign of weakness.

Free Weights

Targets for beginners are: curl 50 per cent body weight, press 70 per cent body weight, squat 100 per cent body weight.

Sarjent Jump

This should exceed 50cm; a jump of more than 65cm is first class.

Step Test

Use a firm box, a metronome – a visual signal is better than a bleeper – and a timer. The step height should be 50cm for men, 45cm for women and 40cm or less (according to age) for juniors.

A severe test is stepping for 5 minutes at a rate of 30 steps per minute. The metronome is set to 120 beats per minute (4 beats per step). After the 5 minutes, rest for 1 minute and count the number of pulse beats in the next 30 seconds.

The fitness index is the time in seconds multiplied by 100, divided by the 30 second pulse count and multiplied by 5.5. An index of 80 to 99 is reasonable, 100 to 119 is creditable, 120 to 139 is good, 140 to 159 is very good, 160 to 179 is excellent, 180 and over is superb.

Height–weight Ratio

Dr Stillman's height–weight ratio for non-running men 1.5m tall gives a weight of 50kg. Add 2.5kg for each additional 2.5cm. The ratio for non-running women of the same height gives a weight of 45kg, plus 2.3kg for each additional 2.5cm.

For men or women in training deduct 10 per cent for their ideal middle distance weight. Long-distance runners are even more meagre in weight. Marathon and 10,000m runners should weigh 20 per cent less than non-runners, 5000m runners 15 per cent less, 1500m runners 10 per cent less and 800m runners 5 per cent less. Notable exceptions were Seb Coe and Rick Wohlhuter, both 1.75m tall and weighing about 60kg.

Percentage Body Fat

This should be less than 8 per cent in men, less than 13 per cent in women. Those seeking quality performances should not exceed these figures.

Muscular Endurance Test

Test the maximum number of press-ups per minute: 30 is poor, 40 is fair, 50 is good.

For squat thrusts the knees must reach the arms: 30 per minute is poor, 40 is fair, 50 is good.

For sit-ups per minute, with legs flat and chin on chest, sliding the hands to the knees: 40 per minute is poor, 50 is fair, 60 is good.

For pull-ups with the palms forward: 3 per minute is poor, 6 is fair, 10 is good, 15 is very good, 20 is excellent.

FLEXIBILITY EXERCISES

Before any flexibility exercises or tests, thoroughly warm up. Stretch both sides of the body. Do not exceed the threshold of discomfort or pain.

Do not bounce or jerk. Induce stretch slowly. If assisted stretching is used great care must be exercised and the assister must know what they are doing. An exception could be ballistic stretching, if considered absolutely necessary.

Maintain stretch stimulus at or near maximum for between 20 and 40 seconds. Check for a difference in flexibility between the left and right sides. Check on injuries – past, present or developing.

A reasonably detailed description of suitable flexibility exercises together with the necessary illustrations would require a small book. A first-class 800m runner, particularly one who has followed a good strength training programme, will possess a well developed musculature and this physique coupled with the demands of the event requires a stretching routine that contributes reasonable injury prevention and ensures a good range of movement.

The full range of movements for the 800m and 1500m must also match the needs of all-out sprinting. The flexibility exercises that hurdlers typically follow will meet these needs and provide an excellent base for a preventive maintenance routine. However, be careful as some hurdling exercises place extra torsion on joints, particularly the knees.

STRENGTH TRAINING

Circuit training and weight training to build up strength are ignored at your peril. There are those who say that strength training is not necessary because they have been successful without it. The answer to them is the same as the answer to those who argue that there is no need to worry about style as the body will naturally develop the style most suited to it: had they followed a carefully constructed remedial programme they would have been even better. It is the same with strength training.

Skeletal Muscles

Before drawing up suggested programmes it is worth considering some of the functions of the skeletal muscles. These muscles are only about 40 per cent of total body weight in men – slightly less in women – and not all of them are agonists (prime movers). It follows that the agonists have a proportionately heavy load to carry around of what could be considered as dead weight.

It is easily demonstrated that against a given load a strong muscle will contract faster than a weaker one, so that within the constraints of producing the optimum mix of strength, suppleness and endurance it is obvious that to maximize performance the athlete should maximize dynamic strength. Strength improves speed through the improved co-ordination that is specific to fast running. While some spin-off in improved co-ordination is one of the benefits of circuit, weight and plyometric training it does not mean that all skills learned from one activity transfer directly to another.

The agonists are those muscles supplying the major part of the force used to perform the necessary movement. They are most effective when they are in perfect co-ordination with their opposing muscles, the antagonists. If during fast running either the quadriceps or the hamstrings do not relax when the other is contracting a frequent result is a muscle tear. At other times and with differing degrees of tension in both they may be called upon to control more subtle movements.

The synergist muscles assist the agonists and their function is also improved by being strengthened. They play a significant role when helping to combat the onset of fatigue. Athletes are often confused about lactate production and its effect. An excess of lactate accumulation can seriously inhibit the activity of the enzymes involved in energy production, but lactate is also a fuel. The important point is that muscles other than the agonists can metabolize lactate. A well-developed general musculature from a carefully thought out circuit and weight training programme is very advantageous in coping with lactate production and accumulation.

Posture

An important function of skeletal muscle is maintaining posture, and this is improved by having good muscle tone. Improved balance and co-ordination make postural work a lot easier. Muscles also help to protect joints from injury and the stronger the muscle the greater the protection.

Bad posture puts unnecessary stress on joints. Many problems, such as low back pain, are associated with poor posture.

Firm muscles with good tone help to avoid such complaints. Another example is having weak adductor muscles to the legs. A sudden sideways slip of one foot while running in wet or icy conditions can keep a runner out of serious training for a long time and adductors are notoriously vulnerable. Correct exercises to strengthen these muscles are a good insurance against the long lay-offs associated with adductor strain.

Muscle Building

Continuing steady work at circuit and weight training ensures an even, all-round development. The tendons are given time to keep up with and match the strengthened muscles. Some athletes, of course, are tempted to use steroids to build up their muscles. Apart from the immorality and any ill-effects on general health, a serious danger with steroids is that their use permits a rapid increase in muscle bulk and strength that is not matched by the tendons. Thus there is a greater risk of tendon rupture. It is always safer to gain strength the slower and honest way.

Other Advantages

In addition to an improvement in strength there are other important physiological gains. The key to muscle function is motor innervation and a motor nerve is made up of many nerve cells. These cells branch out to connect to variable numbers of muscle fibres. A motor unit is a single neuron and all the fibres innervated by it. Strength training develops better functioning of the muscles through improved synchronizing and recruitability of the motor units. Thus there is better team work among motor units and as more units are recruited for submaximal work-loads the muscle can function at a lower intensity.

Put simply, if for the same load more muscle fibres are recruited then each fibre (and thus the whole muscle) is working with less strain. Very quick running demands dynamic leg strength and although retired Seb Coe can still produce very good standing long jumps. This ability is maintained by regular sessions on a leg press of six sets of 20 × 220kg.

To be successful at the highest level a middle distance runner needs to have good, repeatable 400m speed. The 400m is a sprint event at the endurance end of the short speed spectrum, and this accords nicely with the modern concept of the 800m being an extended sprint. Any sprint coach will tell you that over and above the mastery of starting and general technique, the absolute must for really fast work is raw, animal strength.

It was the long and careful attention to strength training that enabled a slightly built Seb Coe to run successfully in 400m events and relays (including 45.5 seconds in the 4 x 400m at the European Cup Final in August 1979 in Turin.) It was not a casual fill-in activity but a carefully thought out, strictly maintained, serious programme that commenced with circuit training to provide the initial all-round strength to safely handle

weights. It was started and kept going for the six years he was at Loughborough. Together with a very good flexibility regime this total physical conditioning was maintained all through his career and continued, in a modified form, in retirement.

Flexibility

As strength is enhanced so must suppleness be improved. To this end assisted stretching such as George Gandy applied to Seb at Loughborough is invaluable, but the assister *must* know what to do and how to do it. It is very easy to over-stretch and hurt an athlete.

A correct weight training programme does not make slow runners. Just think, have you ever seen a successful weight-lifter whose lifts were slow? A clean and jerk or a snatch is just what it is called. Likewise, runners will not become 'muscle bound'. The correct exercises to develop strength and endurance are not those used for producing hypertrophy.

Strength training is not restricted to the winter months, it is an ongoing and essential activity, but it does vary in content and intensity as the training year progresses. It tapers off to no more than very light exercises just before peaking for the athlete's major goal of the year. For that short period only, reduced weight work – enough to maintain racing strength and the flexibility routine – is maintained. Before outlining any schedules some definitions of circuit and stage training are necessary.

Circuit Training and Stage Training

The idea behind circuit training is that at each station an exercise is done that is one of a planned series. The series is so devised and sequenced that when performed consecutively it will stimulate strength, power, stamina, agility, flexibility and cardiopulmonary conditioning. The use of the word circuit derives from the fact that this type of work is most easily done around the walls of a sports hall or gymnasium and the most convenient layout is the one that finishes where the series of exercises started.

Whereas in circuits the number of repetitions at each station is relatively short, stage training uses much longer repetitions at fewer stages or stations. The latter lends itself nicely to forming a basic routine with a few exercises using simple room furniture, which can be easily maintained when away from your usual facility.

When considering the number of repetitions per station or exercise in weight training be aware that progression might on occasion be better achieved as an increase in the number of repetitions per set rather than as an increase in the weight or load handled, especially when working mainly on endurance.

The number of repetitions per station in circuit training may be calculated as follows. For the easier exercises a 60 second period is suitable and for the harder ones a 45 second period is suggested. The maximum number of repetitions that can be performed during each of these periods is established. Next, half the number of these maximum repetitions is assigned to each set of exercises. The number of different exercises, their nature and the duration of the whole session will depend on the level of fitness and experience of the athlete.

Although these sessions can be made extremely arduous, the intent is for the athlete to remain continuously active, be at each station for about the same length of time and not become excessively fatigued. Good technique and speed should be maintained.

The following suggested and generalized routines for circuit and weight training assume that the reader is new to this type of workout. In individual cases there may be a shift of emphasis to correct any major weaknesses that are perceived but the aim, as in the overall training plan, is always to maintain a balance. It is outside the scope of this book to recommend any specific remedial exercises, as these should be prescribed with specialist orthopaedic advice or by a good sports physiotherapist.

Circuit Training

Table 1 caters for the needs of beginners as well as those with some experience of higher levels of all-round strength and fitness. It is compiled to give a comparison between sessions graded as easy, medium and hard respectively. The first footnote mentions eight to twelve exercises although only five to nine are shown in the table. The higher figures are mentioned because they would give a greater

Half squats   Ranging from two sets of 5×200 to two sets of 500 each, with each recovery equal to the duration of one set.

Bent knee sit-ups   Alternating straight trunk curls with oblique trunk curls, alternate elbows touching the opposite knee. Work up to one set of 200 to 250 repetitions.

Press-ups   With the feet elevated to incline the lower limbs, do 5 sets of 20 repetitions.

Back extensions   Using a friend or some heavy piece of furniture like a table to stabilize both legs, 3 or 4×20 to 30 repetitions. Even when proficient, do no more than 100 per session.

Step-ups   Using a box or a low, sturdy table start as follows. Stage 1: ten step-ups on each leg comprises one set; complete four sets. Stage 2: repeat Stage 1, doing twenty step-ups on each leg. Stage 3: increase by steps of ten until forty per leg are achieved. Stage 4: commence working on one leg at a time. Start with sixty continuous steps on each leg and progress in easy stages to one set of a hundred on each leg. Once this level has been reached it is safe to progress to much higher repetitions. This exercise is specific to local muscular endurance. Further increases in easy steps are required for improved performance.

diversity to keep the athlete's interest and at the same time vary the possible combinations of muscle groups to be conditioned. Clearly to perform four or five circuits of twelve stations if all were used with maximum repetitions would be very hard and take a long time.

Stage Training

Although stage training may be done domestically or in a hotel room when travelling instead of in a gymnasium, the phrase still denotes the completion of all the chosen stages. While this type of training serves as an excellent replacement for circuit work when a gym is not available it does lack some of the variety and it does not involve any agility, nor does it engage as many muscle groups.

Nevertheless, it is very useful if the athlete wants to develop specific local muscular endurance. To this end Seb Coe always combined stage and circuit work for part of the year. The panel shows a typical stage set-up and routine that was successfully employed by him for many years.

Stage training can be made as hard or as easy as is thought necessary, commensurate with the progress and development of the athlete and the current period of the training year. It cannot be stressed too often that when a new element or system is introduced the athlete should go carefully and treat it with respect. The old adage about sudden changes in training being risk prone is very true. The best and longest-lasting results invariably come from a smooth progression and not from trying for overnight improvements. These seldom, if ever, occur but are dangerous to attempt.

When doing long repetitions at each stage it is unlikely that the athlete will do – or want to do – more than one circuit, but if the numbers of repetitions are kept low it is appropriate to perform more than one circuit. Athletes are competitive people and exercises can become addictive no matter how hard the work becomes. At all times remember the main objective of a runner's training – to be a better runner, not to be the best weightlifter, rope climber or to break the record for half squats with only body weight. Athletes are naturally competitive people. It is easy to lose sight of the main objective when a group of athletes begin to feel competitive in a group activity such as circuit training in a sports hall.

By all means train hard, but save the controlled aggression that gives the competitive edge for actual racing. When the athlete is experienced enough to make a session of circuits or weights a really hard one it should be the main session of the day, particularly with weight training. Such a session must not be followed by a hard speed endurance or fast long run. The following day should be an easier one, allowing full recovery.

Weight Training

There are some basic safety rules for weight training. It is always important to have the right equipment and assistance when handling weights. Having someone in attendance (it is better to have two spotters) who can either take away the weights or help to support them if you lose control can save you from injury, especially when you may be attempting a maximum lift to assess progress in straightforward strength gains.

A major contribution to safety in any sport is mastering and using the proper technique. Correct breathing when lifting is part of it. The traditional view is to exhale during the action phase and inhale on return. Essentially this is correct but there are also structural and physiological reasons for a modified approach. It is quite appropriate during the maximum effort of the pushing or pulling to hold the breath briefly. This creates a rigid rib cage through an increase in intrathoracic pressure. This and an accompanying increase in tension in the abdominal muscles provide extra support for the thoracic spine.

A good solid lifter's belt should be worn at all times together with a good pair of proper lifter's shoes. Ordinary runner's training shoes, no matter how good, do not provide adequate support or very solid heels. If the right footwear cannot be acquired then it is much better to wear stout, well-fitting walking shoes than trainers.

The seven lifting exercises shown in Table 1 are *not* maximum lifts and are designed to develop strength and endurance. So what are the weights to be employed at each lift? In interval training the best pace to start with is the one that enables you to finish the session – not

Suggestions for comparing light, medium and hard training sessions using circuit, stage and weight training.

The exercises to be performed in each set or circuit are marked with an X	Circuits [a] Number of circuits			Stage training [b] Number of stages		
	2–3 Easy	3–4 Medium	4–5 Hard	5–6 Easy	7–8 Medium	8–10 Hard
Dips		X	X			
Back extensions	X	X		X		
Back extensions over chair		Xc			Xc	Xc
Bent knee sit-ups, straight raise	X			X		
Bent knee sit-ups, twisting raise		X			X	
Bent knee sit-ups, inclined			X			X
Press ups (push ups)	X				X	X
Press ups, feet elevated			X		X	X
Squat thrusts (frog jumps)	X		X	X		
Burpees		X	X		X	X
Leg raise			X			
Rope climb		X	X			
Chin ups (pull ups)	X	X				
Barbell step ups			X	X	X	X

Strength and endurance weight training	Repetitions/set			Sets		
	Easy	Medium	Hard	Easy	Medium	Hard
Barbells curls	2	6	10	3	4	6
Bent-arm pullovers	2	5	8	3	3	2
Barbell bench press	2	4	6	4	4	4
Barbell half-squats	2	4	6	6	6	6
Barbell alternated front lunges	2	4	6	3	6	6
Vertical rowing	2	3	5	4	5	6
Barbell step-ups (moderate load)	10	15	20	2	4	5–6

[a] Each circuit should consist of between 8 and 12 exercises when athlete is fully accustomed to this kind of training.

[b] Each stage is a single exercise done with a given number of repetitions.

[c] Use caution with this exercise if there is any lower-back weakness: as with other exercises, always use care initially.

Table 1 Comparative programmes for circuit, stage and weight training.

easily but well worked without excessive fatigue. Select the starting weight for each exercise in the same way. There will have to be a trial period during which the athlete experiments to find the correct starting weights.

Plyometrics

Those athletes who are able to use a large sports hall for their circuits might wish to incorporate some plyometrics into their conditioning. The main principle behind the use of plyometrics is utilizing the effect of pre-stretching a muscle immediately before contraction. This creates a greater contracting force.

While dramatic gains in dynamic strength are possible it must be said that there is a greater risk of injury. When landing after jumping the muscles must overcome the additional acceleration caused by gravity. This places the muscles under eccentric tension, during which fewer muscle fibres are recruited, increasing the risk of damage to the fibres doing the work.

The simplest plyometric exercise is taking long bounding strides, as practised by triple jumpers and sprinters, but with it go some heavy shock loading and the chance of a turned ankle. Box bounding or jumping consists mainly of continuous jumping over hurdles or low boxes (perhaps just the top sections of vaulting boxes) or jumping from the top of higher boxes to the floor and rebounding back to the same height on the next box – also continuously. The main safety measures here are always to take off and land even-

ly with both feet so that one leg does not take the major part of the load. Because of the increased heights and greater shock on landing there is an extra need for good balance and co-ordination to avoid injury. It is acceptable to land on firm mats but not on anything too soft or unstable. There are no firm rules about commencing heights. They are determined by safety and the athlete's ability.

Experience with distance runners indicates that they tend not to have the same co-ordination and balance as 800m and 1500m runners. The need to practise plyometrics is inversely proportional to the distance of the athlete's main event, although it can have quite a beneficial effect on hill climbing when competing in genuinely hilly cross-country events.

Like any other type of training for running, strength training should be preceded by an adequate warm-up. An easy 3 to 5km run to the gym, or round the block a few times before stage training at home, would do nicely except in very cold weather. Again, complete a good stretching routine before you start and all should be well. Try to maintain your usual easy cool-down to prevent any stiffness, just as you would after any hard running session.

Starting Strength Training

Those using strength training for the first time should start slowly and progressively, and enjoy the general all-round improvement. Beginners will certainly ask how long a session should last. The unhelpful but honest answer is just as

The middle distance events are endurance based events needing speed and strength. Seb Coe weight training at Loughborough.

long as it takes to cover the desired programme. After acquiring enough experience a meaningful session will usually take around 1 to 1½ hours. Some exercises will be harder for some athletes than for others, so the following division of the stations into hard and easy might seem a little arbitrary.

Consider the circuits described as medium in Table 1, in which only seven stations are suggested. Treat the first, second and last as being harder and the rest as being easier. Remember that when it was earlier explained how to assess the number of repetitions in a set the easier ones were half the maximum number

achievable in 1 minute and the harder ones were half those done in 45 seconds.

The recovery between sets is the same as the work time taken by the set, so the time allotted to the work and the recovery adds up to about 19 minutes for three circuits and 25 minutes for four circuits. Allowing 15 seconds to move smartly from station to station – no hanging about or you will lose the anaerobic content of the session – and you will finish with total times for the main activity of between 25 and 32 minutes. On the same basis the times for four to five circuits of the hard session add up to around 40 to 50 minutes. To these totals must be

31

	To Wk	
Mid Oct	4	Complete rest, no running, only light callisthenics and flexibility excercises.
Nov	11	One circuit training or easy stage training session each week.
Dec	15	Two stage sessions, one easy, one hard, each week.
Jan	20	Two stage training sessions, both hard, each week.
Feb light	24	One moderate stage session and one easy weight session, using weights for endurance, each week.
Mar	28	One moderate stage session and one endurance weight session, using heavier weights, each week.
Apr	32	One week of hard endurance weight sessions alternating with one week of pyramid lifting reaching 90–95% max.
May	37	One endurance weight session and one easy stage session each week.
Jun	41	Alternating weeks of one easy endurance weight session with one easy stage or circuit training session.
Jul	45	One easy circuit or stage session each week.
Aug	50	Competition period, mobility work only.
Mid Sep	52	Competiton period, mobility work only.

Table 2   Easier programme for strength training.

added the proper warm-up, stretching and flexibility exercises and a little run-off.

However, these figures only explain the ideal situation. Although the athlete performs only half the maximum number of repetitions at each station it is very unlikely that as the session progresses the time taken to do these exercises will be kept to the theoretical times allowed, as the athlete inevitably tires. This alone will significantly increase the overall times. One can easily see that such sessions can be as hard or as easy as you need and the

Mid	To	/Wk	
Oct	4		Complete rest, no running, only light callisthenics and flexibility exercises.
Nov	11		One easy stage/circuit session plus one easy weight session each week.
Dec	15		One medium stage/circuit session plus one medium weight session each week.
Jan	20		Two easy stage/circuit sessions plus one medium weight session each week.
Mar	28		One medium stage/circuit session and one hard weight session each week.
Apr	32		One medium stage/circuit session plus one session of endurance weight lifting per week. The lifting alternates weekly with pyramid lifting reaching 90–95% max.
May	37		One easy stage/circuit session and one hard weight session each week.
Jun	41		One medium stage/circuit session per week alternating with one medium weight session per week.
Jul	45		One easy stage/circuit per week alternating with one easy weight session per week.
Aug	50		Competition period. One easy weight session per week.
Mid Sep	52		End of competition period and extra conditioning work.

Table 3   Harder programme for strength training.

same is true of both stage training and weight training. Do not be afraid of really hard work in the gym but start slowly and safely and try to make the work progressive. The examples given of recovery times are not those of the weight room, where the whole tempo of the work is slower and there are extra safety precautions.

Table 2 is designed to fit in with a single periodization table. It is drawn up carefully, almost over-cautiously, to be suitable for beginners and those runners who have not previously been on a comprehensive strength and conditioning course.

For those who have experience of handling weight training this table has a weakness, as the weight training ceases too soon in the training year. For longer distance runners this might not be so serious but for middle distance athletes needing good 400m strength and speed the extra weight training could be crucial to getting the best results.

For this more experienced group Table 3 is preferred. It continues weight training into the competitive season. I have direct experience of the need to follow this latter course when preserving speed and strength through to the end of a long season and the last of the big grand prix meetings.

The reason for this is that if strength declines so will 400m speed. It is stated that after a three-month lay-off from regular weight training there may be as much as a 30 per cent loss of strength. An athlete maintaining a good programme of stage and circuit work will of course be doing a form of strength training, so the fall off will be reduced. Furthermore, a runner will still be exercising his or her legs when racing and training. However, because being only half of 1% below your best is enough to take you from the front to the back of the field in a hard-fought, class race, maintaining strength and speed is crucial to success.

To continue to improve and reach the target all training must be progressive if the athlete is to avoid habituation. Just as times and distances progress on the track, so must the performances in the gymnasium and weight room improve. Progression can be an increase in any one or combination of the following sessions:

- Weights or an improvement in times
- Duration or the number of repetitions in sets
- The number of sets in a session
- A reduction in the recovery times between intervals
- A reduction in the recovery times between sets

≡3≡
MENTAL CONDITIONING

MENTAL CONDITIONING TO TRAINING AND COMPETITION

The best place to start is always the beginning, and the sooner the better. In home life the child with an 'early to bed and early to rise' upbringing that includes all homework and chores being finished before play will have, through this early discipline, a head start over those who have not had this advantage. Were it possible to make this choice, the best advice that could be given to any child would be to choose its mother carefully! They can lay the best foundation for later life.

Whether coaching young beginners or experienced runners the coach must emphasize from the outset that punctuality for all training or racing sessions is essential. Apart from accidents or illness, any failure to turn up or complete the recommended sessions will not be tolerated. For everyone's benefit, particularly the athlete's, attending more attractive dates or events must result in censure. If these rules are frequently broken then the ath-

lete's relationship with the coach must be terminated.

The following is an important example of discipline, because it involves a very keen and dedicated athlete and not a less committed runner. A common mistake in the attitude to injury is the attempt to return to training and competition too soon. This is best shown in the way athletes ask a key question. It should not be 'How soon can I start running again?' The proper approach is to ask 'How long must I rest before it is safe to resume training?' It is an example of when restraint needs discipline just as much as facing up to hard racing and training does.

Coaches and athletes must be able to discuss frankly any causes for worry – real or imaginary – particularly those of health. This includes not only current injuries but any problem that they feel may be impending before the start of any training session or race. For female athletes this means they should not allow undue modesty to prevent full and frank

800m running demands a fast pace and a relaxed style at speed, both shown by Seb Coe here in a race at Crystal Palace he went on to win.

discussion of any physical condition that could inpair their training or racing. The coach should be advised of any medical advice that is relevent to training, and attempt to minimise embarassment.

Failing to fulfil a schedule just because the athlete does not feel like it is a form of cowardice. No runner can be lucky enough to turn up to every competition feeling in perfect condition and ready to give a first-class performance. There will always be the odd occasion when a runner has to honour a commitment, and it is no use going to the start full of feelings of defeat and without a firm resolution to do the very best you can. Always carrying out training to the full develops the will, and resistance to ceding victory too easily. The last thing an athlete needs is a feeling of defeat to intrude before a race.

A classic example for me was in 1975 when Seb Coe was entered for the Northern Counties 3000m Junior Championship at Blackburn. Although previously he had been enthusiastic about the race, when he arrived at the track he was very uncertain about competing. He made what was for him a rare comment that he was not feeling up to it. After a long talk with him and an assessment of his condition I could not figure out how real or serious the problem was, other than the fact that he felt down and below par.

While turning this over in my mind I met another coach, Gordon Surtees, whom I knew quite well. I mentioned my predicament. He thought for a bit, sympathized and admitted that it was not an easy decision to make but finished with

the following canny remark: 'He is a good athlete but he will not go through his career always feeling like racing.' The answer was right there, and by hurrying I just got in Seb's entry in time for acceptance.

After Seb trailed further and further behind the leader, a very good athlete, the race looked hopelessly lost with only one lap to go. From the track side I roared: 'That's far enough, go, go, go.' With an astonishing last lap and a storming finish Seb just got up on the line to steal the race. That one race has provided us with a rallying cry for any situation, even all these years later. Whenever the going gets tough all that is needed is: 'Remember Blackburn.'

The race was a triumph of mind over matter, and the moral here is one that we have never forgotten. It is to never form bad habits; they may return quite unexpectedly and when least desired. But of course if the worry is a genuine one then the rule is simple: *if in doubt, don't.* Injuries are more easily acquired than cured.

A PROFESSIONAL APPROACH

It follows that if the coach is to demand and obtain high standards from athletes, his or her own personal and professional standards should be above reproach. A coach is honoured by the athlete's choice just as much as the athlete is by the coach's accepting the responsibility. A professional attitude should be developed and maintained throughout a career. Professionalism is too often and too easily dismissed as simply performing for money, whereas it should be thought of as working with dignity, diligence and care.

This attitude should encompass all aspects of the training session. The session can be strongly influenced by the presence of others who, if they are the wrong people, can affect the concentration of the athlete, and therefore that of the coach, to the detriment of the session.

In growing up, one measure of maturity is how well a person understands the difference between work and play. This may show in athletes by the people they invite to be present when they are training. Dour though this may sound, a serious training session is not the place for socializing with loved ones or admiring friends. They cannot help and are only a distraction, often to the coach as well. They may have their place, but that has to come in the legitimate leisure time for necessary relaxation.

As when laying down any other training conditions, especially those that might not at first seem reasonable, close and sympathetic communication is required. There can only be reasoned explanations – seldom, if ever, concessions. The hard demands imposed by the ultimate goal are such that the coach cannot offer an easy route to success. The athlete must appreciate that what he wants will exact a high price.

The good side of all this is when the big wins start to come. For a short and heady moment the daily grind is forgotten, the coach is thanked and forgiven, and further success beckons. For the true winner, there is nothing like winning.

Sometimes the system under which young athletes operate puts them with a personality not suitable for their present level of physical or personal development. This might have to be borne until they can either join another organization or become mature enough to find good alternative advice, meanwhile extracting what they can from the immediate situation. Guidance from a mature adult who is knowledgeable about their sport is another option, but one cannot follow two coaches. This is not meant to be granting permission for changing coaching advice every time they feel like it – those who frequently chop and change reveal more about themselves than about the coaching.

Somewhat different conditions exist for the more experienced runner. In choosing or accepting a coach the athlete must be prepared to obey the coach's instructions about time, place and session. Each and every athlete is an experiment of one and in any experiment the control is lost by varying more than one factor at a time. Therefore it is essential for success that when away from the coach the athlete carries out any instructions honestly and carefully, or the relationship will not work without mutual trust. It would be better to sever the relationship than to waste time in recrimination.

Never forget that effective communication must work both ways: it is the only way to avoid misunderstandings. Desirable and essential as the above discipline is it cannot be voluntarily obtained if the coach is not, if asked, able

For later success, early toughening exercises – both mental and physical – are necessary. Sand dune running is a particularly demanding exercise.

and prepared to explain the reasoning behind all the demands of the training. This conditioning is continuous and has a significant physical component. (See The Training Programme.)

THE WILL TO WIN

The true winner is highly goal-oriented and has learned very early on that participation and winning are not the same. The latter may come only after the former, but it does not follow automatically; a win has to be won. Really great and consistent winners – not those who just get lucky on the odd day – are those whose only satisfaction, and a temporary one at that, comes from success. There might be some comfort in the knowledge that the last training session reached a new and higher level, but it is more like-

ly that any satisfaction will come from winning a hard race that they know was significant. Do not be ashamed to believe that *if winning is not everything then it very nearly is.*

This is not the antithesis of sport but the essence of competition, to be earnestly pursued while strictly observing the rules of the game to the letter and spirit. Cheating, whether by drug abuse or in any other form, is a major detriment to athletes because with it they embark on the steep and slippery slope of self-doubt. They are admitting to themselves that they are not really the best, and this knowledge will eat away at them and ultimately undermine their resolve. Meanwhile, they prefer dishonesty to decency.

A great athlete should be proud of his or her success, and genuine pride is a great sustainer when under pressure. When faced with the choice of running for money or running for excellence, pride should be on the side of excellence. The best athletes readily understand that while excellence might produce a lot of money, money can never replace excellence, although it frequently spoils it. So often we have heard 'I would give anything to have won an Olympic medal.' Chasing money all too frequently involves over-racing and there are those who must feel that they have left their medal chances behind somewhere on the grand prix circuit. When it is not enhancing your development, pressure to compete, from any source, *must be strongly resisted.*

Even if all other competitors have been beaten, the true champion will still be left racing against himself or herself for that ever-elusive pinnacle of excellence. In a television interview David Coleman commented to Seb Coe that some runners were motivated by the opposition, and asked: 'But you seem to be self-motivated, how do you do it?' The reply was: 'I suppose it is the motivation of just wanting to go out and run faster than I have run before, and hopefully faster than any one else has run, and that gives me a lot of pleasure. It is sitting down before a race and feeling that at the end of the evening I may have achieved something really special.'

Real champions love their sport dearly for its own sake. They recognize the value of participation, with its comradeship and support from their clubmates, but appreciate that it can never provide or

replace the deeper satisfaction of success – or satisfy the hunger for it.

Debates concerning their motivation are academic, because these real champions are driven by a very high self-image. They perceive themselves as being very successful, real winners, the best. They pursue the goal of being number one with a single-minded determination to be nothing less.

What great runners often achieve is total domination of their events. Their level of performance becomes so intimidating that the rest of the runners know that at best they are only competing for second place. The following is an extract from a paper in the February 1980 copy of the 'Olympian', by J.R.May Associate Professor of Psychiatry and Behavioural Sciences, School of Medical Sciences, University of Nevada:

'Sports psychologists agree its the rare top athlete who goes all out to be the number one. Rather, within his or her field, they strive to excel, and in the excelling he wins a variety of world class honours.'

Two thoughts arise from this. The first is that it may account for there being very few who come to dominate totally in their event, and the second is that the earlier a genuine talent is encouraged to adopt the belief that he or she could dominate as number one, the sooner and greater is their chance of achieving it.

The great champions also have the vital ability to focus all their aggression into this will to win, and yet remain normal and relaxed outside competition. Before the start of a race they distance themselves from all that is happening around them and take on a look that is a strange mix of detachment and concentration. Seb Coe always did it, and in the 1992 Barcelona Olympics and the following World Championships the cameras perfectly captured that special look on Linford Christie's face just before he won the gold medal.

This quality of being able to be single-minded is often manifested in their post-athletic careers. And it does not go away. After Seb Coe's retirement I was reviewing the 1992 season with him, and I commented on a superlative run by a fine new athlete. I said: 'At 800m he would not have troubled you but at 1500m you would have had your work cut out to hold him.' The reaction was instantaneous; the old glint of battle shone in his eyes and with total conviction and confidence he said: 'When I was at my best – no bother.' It is not arrogance that I am describing, it is total belief in yourself. In short, the *best will not yield to the rest.*

My insistence on early, strict compliance with legitimate instructions is not merely to enforce slavish obedience but, as early as possible, to strengthen the steely will to succeed. The ultimate expression of this is, as Seb did, to go to the start of an Olympic final knowing it is your day and quietly saying to yourself: 'This is my title and not one of you is going to get it!'

On big occasions a good coach's duties are mainly those of a specialized valet. Any discussion about the race should have been over much earlier. All the irritating chores of bag carrying, checking in for the race, checking if the programme is running late and preventing a premature warm-up – all these and more are the job of the coach. Intelligent and dedicated athletes will appreciate this attention to detail at all times, and feel that the coach is doing the job thoroughly and not merely fussing.

This is a very important part of coaching and it is the first step in showing an athlete of any age that in return for dedication and discipline the coach will be, at all times and in every way, totally supportive of the runner and his or her ambition.

REINFORCEMENT

Although powerfully motivated athletes carry a high image of themselves it does not follow that when they are young they always feel secure, nerveless and not in need of care and support. Young people need to know that there is someone on whom they can depend totally when facing all the setbacks that happen along the way. Correct support and understanding during these early years are vital in developing the ability to cope with the much greater problems and setbacks that even the best encounter at the height of their careers.

Reinforcement of this drive should be carried on throughout their competitive careers and especially in their final years as mature champions, although with a more subtle and refined approach. Really effective encouragement will work only if, at all times, the coach is totally honest with the athlete – difficult though this

41

may be. This way the athlete always knows that any praise or encouragement from the coach is genuine and any adverse criticism is well worth heeding. Sometimes comment may have to be cruel to be kind but it must never be merely negative – it must always be specific and informative.

As long as a fair and accurate analysis of any fault or error is given, there is nothing wrong with making it a little more palatable by referring an athlete to their better performances and assuring them that they can still repeat them, and do even better. If the race or the training session is a bad one it must be clearly stated, but the appropriate corrective work must also be indicated.

If all has gone extremely well then it is in order to give some warm praise, but not accompanied by rash forecasts of further instant success. Reinforcing runners' belief in themselves is not as easy as it might seem. It is most important, especially with juniors, that when forecasting future achievements you simultaneously stiffen their will.

Explain that as the catchment area of the opposition rapidly increases so will the standards and the records. They need to be prepared for this. From a school sports day to an Olympic gold is a very long way. This way they are encouraged to think big and at the same time be conditioned to cope with the fact that the better they get the harder it always becomes. It is hard to get to the top; it gets harder all the time staying there. Anything less than their ultimate ambition is only another rung on a ladder, leading up

from School then District and Area, then National and European Championships, to World and Olympic Golds. A journey during which the opposition grows from hundreds to many millions. It bears repeating that this is still not the end of the road, because ultimately the very best champions are still left competing against themselves.

As soon as it is at all feasible, have a sheet on which forecasts of times, events, championships and even world records together with their respective estimated achievement dates are listed. The coach and the athlete can in time sit down and tick them off and share the mutual satisfaction. The coach can then give some well deserved praise and any guarded but well founded expectations of further progress that are appropriate. After all, *nothing succeeds half as much as success.*

For the powerfully motivated athlete winning is the strongest incentive to even greater victories. Winning also reinforces the athlete's belief in the correctness of the coaching. This conviction that the training is correct gives a very potent boost to the athlete's self-confidence and to his or her confidence in the coach.

There are other ways of quietly and continually reinforcing the athlete's confidence and will to win, one of which is to use a positive nickname. If the athlete is frequently addressed as 'champ' or by some other positive name – particularly after a good training session or a meaningful win – it helps to promote and sustain their essential high personal image and at the same time emphasize the confidence of their coach in them. Without diminishing their impact by indiscriminate use, phrases such as 'Great, you are on target' or 'I felt very proud of you today' or 'You really deserved that win' will have a positive and cumulative effect. If the coach has always been honest these words will be believed. Sooner or later, a runner will always realize if he or she is being conned, and that is very damaging.

Much can be written about encouragement and reinforcement, but whatever methods are used they should be contained in the creation of a strong bond between the coach and athlete and often within a quiet and serious atmosphere when training. Happily there is some comic relief in running, but try and save it for after the sessions. It can sometimes be very difficult to regain concentration.

For the very dedicated coach, life is one long process of eating, sleeping and scheming in pursuit of victory and success, in which no stone is knowingly left unturned. This type of coaching will be seen by some as too obsessive, but it is the only form of truly total commitment that I know and understand. Unless the coach shows this passion and commitment it is not certain that the athlete will. An athlete more committed than the coach will probably leave, and find a coach who is totally committed.

I have shown that these methods can work very well and the pitfalls – which exist in any scheme – can be avoided, although sometimes they have to be experienced and overcome. There is one proviso: much depends on the athlete's intelligence and capacity for rational thought. The athlete must be just as dedicated as the coach but as much as possible must avoid any tension, especially outside of competition. If the coach has proved to be competent and reliable in dealing with all the frictions off the track, the smart athlete will let the coach take the load. Hence earlier comments on an athlete's intelligence.

Going for gold medals and world records means working very close to the limit. In middle distance training it is intensity and not volume that is the most important – so it is with planning. It is the depth of thought and vision that matters, not just a lot of talk and the constant repetition or rehashing of yesterday's received ideas and clever-sounding technical expressions. That is merely 'management by incantation' and it achieves nothing.

Racing against the clock is simply a matter of beating or not beating a time. If in defeat one achieves a personal best time, some might not consider this as losing, whereas head-to-head racing in straight competition can result only in victory or defeat. Setting out to beat everyone in the race is a deliberate and aggressive action and at the top level all the running skill and ability will not avail if it is not matched with an intense aggression directed at winning.

This is not merely blind hostility to everything around, but a clearly focused concentration on the immediate task to the exclusion of anything else. The desire is not only to win but to stamp your authority on the race – in so doing the great champions acquire a reputation and an aura of invincibility. Remember, *when the very best step onto the track the rest know*

43

they are competing for the minor places.

For the true perfectionists it is more than just winning: it is how they win that matters. Coming first with a poor performance leaves them unsatisfied. This driving ambition is beautifully expressed in a quotation used by Frank Dick and taken from *Macbeth:* 'Thou wouldst be great; art not without ambition; but without the illness should attend it.' The word 'illness' emphasizes the driving and almost consuming hunger for success.

There are those who will say that the following examples of the lack of that all-or-nothing drive are hard and somewhat unfair, but I believe they are very revealing. When told of difficulties over obtaining sponsorship my advice is the same as I give to those seeking selection: give them a performance they cannot refuse! Some runners, on no more than a good placing in cross-country or road races, are asking for support grants to allow them to pursue full-time training.

In Oslo in 1979 Seb Coe, already the European Indoor Champion in a very fast time, approached the agent of a major shoe manufacturer for some free kit and was turned down. Later that day, on that same track, he broke the first of his 800m world records and the same agent hurtled across the track to sign him up before anyone else could get to him. I am not suggesting that a world record is the least that is necessary before useful and deserved assistance can be given but that something substantial in the way of showing potential must be shown before expecting reasonable assistance to be given.

A not uncommon attitude of some of our best runners when competing for major titles and championships is that it is acceptable not to win, as long as they come away with a personal best or even just a good time. Following up soon after with a modest win at a lesser domestic meeting, they seem satisfied with their results. That is quite wrong – feeling any satisfaction in such a situation will only limit greater achievement. Sometimes this may be due in part to believing pre-event over-praising or some of the media hype, often too early in their careers, and not accepting genuine informed criticism that is worth listening to. It is also very negative thinking to be contemplating personal records when a major title is at stake. It is the resort of the runner who is settling for the best placing he can get and not that of the athlete who will go for broke!

Such records are best achieved with even-paced running, which is a luxury not found in most great competitive fields. It is acceptable as a tactic only if a pace can be set that will run the rest of the field off their feet. It usually involves front running, which the rest will be happy to let you do. Apart from marathons and some 10km races there are few opportunities to do this successfully, and it is only the gifted and very confident who can pull it off.

I was involved with two Olympic 1500m gold medals, and both would have been lost had the force of Seb Coe's will to win been mixed up and weakened by thoughts of a personal best – which neither race produced although the second final in 1984 set the current Olympic record. It is far better to plan very early

Seb Coe broke his third World Record in 41 days when winning the 1500 metres at Zurich on 15 August 1979. A great athlete shows his respect for a great supportive crowd.

on to remedy any deficiencies in speed and speed endurance, and compete with a full quiver of tactical arrows.

AGGRESSION

When reading these observations on ambition and aggression do not be confused about the limits and containment of this aggression in terms of track behaviour. Competitors must not try to resolve problems created by their own tactical mistakes by using force to extricate themselves from a bad position or to obtain a more desirable place held by another. However, competitors occupying positions fairly obtained can very vigorously defend their spaces in the field. The message will soon get around that they are not to be messed with.

Promoters pack middle distance races with fields that are too large and create major problems, but there is also too much incompetence and unnecessary bad behaviour on the track, particularly in 800m events. This is ignored by judges and comfortably dismissed by some as something to be expected in middle distance events. I am not for one moment suggesting unnecessary meekness in the face of unacceptable track behaviour, but be sure that the nature of your defence is not counter-productive. Some physical contacts can lose too much ground and ruin any chance of winning. Think on your feet and stay smart. In these situations it is once again discipline that is so essential, this time as a safeguard against acting rashly. Always remember that *aggression has to be contained before it can be sharply focused into winning.*

Seeking Success

Pursuit of the cherished number one spot sets an athlete off on a very hard road to follow. He or she will find that winning does not come from superb fitness alone: it also requires a lot of thought, a willingness to make unlimited sacrifices within the bounds of sanity and an unwavering faith that the end is achievable and that the top step of the podium and the winner's laurels are attainable. This too has to be the coach's conviction; a mere dream is not powerful enough to sustain the effort required to reach this goal. No wish or desire is enough in itself; it requires a tremendous act of will. *Mental conditioning must include learning to be pressure-proof in so many ways.*

One definition of success could be 'winning all the greatest prizes in your chosen field of endeavour'. For the athlete in pursuit of excellence it may well be getting as close to perfection as is humanly possible. But with the hungry great, sometimes it is not enough, even when in possession of Olympic gold medals and world records, because between them and the deep satisfaction they seek is the thought that they can, or could, do even better.

Seeking success is one thing; getting it is another. Success has to be lived for, fought for and even breathed for. Every deep breath in a hard training session must give the feeling of inhaling the magic air of success. Success is caught only with unremitting pursuit; once caught it is very difficult to hold, and it is never permanently captured. It will always find a way of slipping from your grasp. Its recapture is a measure of the great champion.

On individual occasions luck can adversely affect the outcome – an infection might take its toll or a clumsy runner might trip another – but in the long run luck is not a factor. Those described as lucky by the envious or the less knowledgeable turn out to have made their own luck – their talent and very hard work are mistaken for luck. Considering their share of ill health and injury, does any serious follower of athletics believe that the careers of Al Oerter, Lasse Viren, Seb Coe, Carl Lewis or Sergey Bubka were the result of luck and not resolution?

IS IT WORTH IT?

I have often been asked this question and my reply is always that it is – for some, but not always for others. Perhaps some of my earlier thoughts on motivation might throw a little light on it. In 1983 in the book *Running for Fitness* I wrote the following:

It does take guts to continue once you have reached the top. Outside observers always seem to be hooked on the motivation problem. After a world record, an Olympic Gold, or whatever strikes them as the pinnacle of success, they all ask: 'What is left to strive for? What can motivate him now?' This success brings with it another problem.

What is hard, and can only get harder all the time, is winning. Not the effort of maintaining the training – that's bad enough – but knowing that

there can never be an unbroken chain of victories. Retiring undefeated looks nice on the record books, but if it is premature, purely to get that distinction, then it does not mean quite so much. Every class athlete knows that the last win he has just notched up takes him one race closer to defeat. One man's forty-five consecutive wins only makes the forty-sixth more desperate.

A world record makes defeat in the same event even more 'inexcusable' at the next championship. There were two winners in the Moscow Olympic Games, of whom after all the adulation, it can be said that only they know the true cost of their Golds.

Olympic titles and World Records go on exacting a price long after the world thinks they have been paid for. There is a common bond between champions and outlaws – they both have a big price on their heads. Carrying that pressure is every bit as tough as the training that keeps them there. Seb Coe: 'I put up with it because I still like winning enough to endure the training. It is nice to have your body working like a well oiled machine, but it is nicer not to go training in mid-winter in the early morning and the late evening with your eyes and ears frozen.'

But there is a magic on the big nights that is very hard to describe, for the alchemy of the spectacular in Zurich, say, or Brussels is at the same time both brutal and subtle. The interviews with the press and television, the media's incessant hunger for the dramatic announcement like 'It's a record attempt tonight' or 'I've come here to win the big one' is a maddening part of the scene one could do well without, but without which it wouldn't be the same. The siege of autograph hunters and the genuine fans, who can make you climb fences to find rear exits from the arena, is only just bearable.

SPORTS PSYCHOLOGY

Psychology often suffers from being thought of as an exact science. While it requires much organized study and subtlety it is not a science in the strictest sense. No theory can be proved to be true: you can only say that no test has been devised to prove it wrong. A true science has to pass this test, whereas not all the assumptions of psychology are submitted to it.

One of the problems that modern society has created is the quasi-religious belief that there is a scientific or technological solution to all your problems. Many will leave their physicians feeling cheated if, instead of being given a prescription for pills, they are given only careful attention and a good evaluation of their needs. So it is I fear with many who expect too much and look to sports psychology for quick fix and a short cut to great performances. In fact it needs thought and application by the athlete to obtain any benefit.

Much of what is written on sports psychology centres around performing well in team games. But team games can be pursued reasonably successfully with the team members having quite different motives for competing, which are not applicable to the highly individual sport of competitive running. In team games the greater number of variables makes it easy,

and attractive, to blame a poor showing on others. Performing well on the track is a very different matter. You might win races when better runners make tactical errors, and there are sometimes genuine accidents, but you have only yourself to blame if you lose.

Writings on sports psychology often cover profiling of mood states, though a good coach in close and sympathetic contact with an athlete will have picked up all the signs of changes in moods and started any necessary corrective work quite early, without the need to formalize it. As with any subjects that are part art, part science, tread carefully and selectively. Some of this chapter could be considered as simple psychology. I prefer to think of it as logic, based on experience and observing much world-class running, but call it what we may, careful thinking about what we do is vital to success.

Particularly for the successful competitor, the track in a big stadium is always a very lonely place. Beyond the reach of coach or guru, from then until the finish, the athlete is quite alone. Therefore, while using whatever can be gained from sports psychology, the athlete must never become addicted and too dependent on counselling or on rigid mental (autogenic) rehearsals.

Analysing the sources of a powerful motivation is not easy, and even if it were always possible to uncover all its roots, or lack of them, it is beyond the scope of this book. Psychology requires us to accept many assumptions, whereas athletes and coaches feel the need to be factual. This short comment on the subject as it applies to middle distance runners precludes any attempt at a deeper analysis. Therefore for practical purposes it is possible to indicate the force of the motivation only by considering the strength of the drive created by the motive.

This is revealed by the volume and intensity of the training to which the giants of the modern sport willingly submit. The details of the hard all-year-round regimes that they undergo in the pursuit of their chosen goals enable us to grasp their single-minded pursuit of the top spot and the power of their will. Any discussion of sports psychology for runners should take into account the long years of mental conditioning required for the success that the physical training should simultaneously and equally provide.

A careful objective assessment of how well the athlete understands the training, accepts the discipline, and is prepared to make reasoned sacrifices over a long period – maybe ten years or more – to reach the number one spot will provide a good indicator of his or her chances of substantial success.

The best coaches are those who can recognize a basic talent early on and develop this genetic endowment successfully, through carefully applied progressive training, into a race-winning ability. They will not claim that they can put in what nature left out. I have long thought that the fierce, driving hunger for competitive success may be more genetic than environmental and perhaps it too may not be put in if not already there. I am not saying that confidence or the wish to succeed cannot be enhanced – that would be denying the effect of environment – only that *the best seem to have an inborn extra drive that is often shown in early childhood.*

Muscle and Mind

A simplified view of this is temporarily to divide the athlete's resources into two categories: muscle and mind. Correct training is hard and progressive, and an athlete can go a long way on a good physique and superb fitness. But to reach his or her maximum potential the athlete must acquire the ability always to be in complete mental control when training, in pre-competition time and during the fiercest of racing. The outcome of major championships often rests on whose is the strongest will. However, there are some techniques that are well worth mastering. They are basically quite simple but if they are found to be difficult you should obtain experienced help.

Autogenic Aids

Control over relaxation can be difficult for the highly motivated. If relaxation is a problem then by all means learn good relaxation techniques or any others you are convinced will help you, but are without risk in your case. At any time the best form of relaxation is untroubled sleep.

The body's circadian rhythms govern the release of hormones, though the timing is different for the two sexes. It has been argued that sleep at the wrong time can upset these cycles, but in fact most of us find that a short nap is quite refreshing. The technique of lying down somewhere quiet and comfortable for a brief sleep can be learned. The art of readily falling asleep as required takes time to learn, but can be of benefit. National championships might take place in the early afternoon, whereas a grand prix event on the international circuit might be run in the late evening.

Once you are asleep it is a near perfect relaxation and autogenic aid, and this is a technique well worth learning. But bear in mind that a state of over-relaxation is hard to snap out of, and failing to achieve the desired relaxation is very irritating and disconcerting. Always make sure that you are awake in good time for pre-race preparation.

Like every exercise or training session, mental tricks can have their disadvantages if not practised correctly or if they are wrongly selected for a particular event – for instance, the wrong kind of visualizing before middle distance races. Sprints and the highly technical field events have sequences of well defined movements that are accurately spaced and timed. These events lend themselves to this kind of mental rehearsal. With other events, such as middle distance racing, which contain many wide-ranging variables, it can prove disastrous. Try making a permutation of all the possibilities that can occur as a middle distance race unfolds and then attempt to list them in the right order. Now can you be quite sure that you will not flounder if what you have so carefully visualized and mentally rehearsed does not happen as foreseen?

Despite any difficulties that might arise in the course of learning certain mental techniques, learning to relax is vital. Difficult or not, the correct degree of relaxation must be achieved. Mental tension creates tension in the muscles that is energy consuming and wasteful – which is why proper pre-race relaxation is so important. Also, the wrong kind of nervous tension tends to inhibit the smooth muscular co-ordination that is a hallmark of good running.

A form of visualization that has worked well with some athletes is seeing themselves experiencing a surge of strength at a pre-selected point in their event. This of course is not the same as visualizing particular incidents or sequences of events.

One of the secrets of sustained fast running is relaxation at speed. This art is not easy to acquire because while the body must not be tense the brain must stay totally alert throughout the race. Also, when the athlete is pressured the brain must not send out any panic signals that cause the runner to tie up. The ultimate test of whether or not the athlete has mastered this art is if he or she can maintain good form right through to the end of a hard fought race. As with style, it is about not losing form when under pressure.

Before going to the start line the athlete must be sufficiently aroused to be alert, aggressive and eager to compete, with sharp concentration on the coming performance. There must be no hangover from the previous hour or two of relaxation from which the athlete must emerge

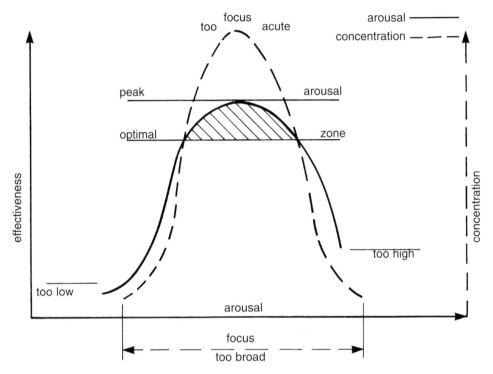

Fig 2   Diagram of arousal, focus and concentration.

fresh and neither drowsy nor with any feelings of weariness.

To compete fiercely the athlete must be aroused, but arousal has its problems too. If it is too low the athlete will not be concentrating sufficiently, but if it is too high an unwelcome anxiety about the outcome of the race will creep in. To be effective this concentration must not be too broad; as one of the most important elements of competition it must be on essentials only. In other words the concentration needs to be focused. The relationship between arousal and focus is interdependent (see Figure 2) and the interaction of the two needs to be optimized in order to achieve the best competition result.

Mental conditioning is more than learning to cope with mental pressure and physical stress: it is also learning to harness the most powerful force we have. Ultimately, successful running is a conquest of the body by the mind.

Shakespeare has supplied one quote on the quest for being great. Now another is borrowed from *Julius Caesar* to make a fitting end to this chapter: 'Men at some time are masters of their fates: the fault, dear Brutus, is not in our stars, but in ourselves.'

=4=
EFFICIENCY, STYLE AND TECHNIQUE

A simple definition of running is to move on foot at a rapid pace so that both feet are off the ground together at some part of the stride. Although it seems such a natural thing to do, it does have to be learned and this seemingly natural motion contains many complex elements. Long after a small child is strong enough to stand up it still cannot walk because it simply has not learned how. Its brain has not yet acquired the complex patterns of how walking is done and how to process the continual flow of information that this requires. These patterns (or templates as they are sometimes called) have to be acquired for every movement that we learn and, within our physical limits, we have the capacity to refine them continually. Luckily, there seems to be little or no mental limit to our ability to absorb new patterns and skills.

An important function of a coach is to be constantly on the lookout for any defect creeping into an athlete's running skill, so that a fault does not intrude into

the ideal pattern. A first-class runner is one who has practised the fundamental skill of running until all the elements that make up the continuous movements of running become so refined that their execution is automatic rather than voluntary. This is exemplified by Seb Coe's reply when he was asked how he felt during his first world record in an 800m race: 'It was wonderful, I was running on auto-pilot.' When these skills have been fully mastered the athlete runs smoothly and elegantly (style) and with the maximum economy (efficiency). The two are complementary.

EFFICIENCY

There are several synergistic components to overall efficiency of which style is one. A runner should not carry around any more fat than is necessary for health. For any given leg length and its ratio to overall height, there will be an optimum stride length for maximum efficiency.

This stride length is modified by dynamic leg strength and the runner's speed.

The runner's level of cardiopulmonary development will determine his or her maximum oxygen uptake (often referred to as VO_2 max), and the mix of fast and slow twitch muscle fibres may set the athlete's range of events. The level reached in developing the ability to buffer acidosis (high acidity in the blood) will limit how far the athlete can run all-out. Improved muscle fibre innervation through correct weight training will, for a given load, reduce the stress on the muscles.

All the above sets the limit of how long and how close to maximum pace the athlete can run. This limit is the ultimate index of efficiency. Maximum efficiency will be lowered by any wasteful expenditure of energy, which is why style is so important.

STYLE

An excellent style is not just an aesthetic and subjective judgement, it is the visual confirmation that the runner has eliminated wasteful movements. The acquisition of a fine style is very important in the early development of an athlete and such remedial work must be continued with the new style until the old faults do not return even when under pressure. Looking at style can be a good diagnostic tool.

A well-poised head presents an unobstructed airway in the throat and removes unnecessary strain from the supporting neck muscles. Too much forward leaning of the trunk is an indication that the runner is compensating for restricted mobility around the hip joints. An early toe-off diminishes stride length and a poor foot plant is not merely unaesthetic, it is very likely indicative of biomechanical problems and the need for podiatric analysis. There might be a need for carefully prescribed orthotics.

Excessive contra-rotation of the upper body, which should never be any more than slight, is unnecessarily fatiguing. A tight, high carriage of the arms affects distance runners in two ways: it is tiring and it works against developing the good sprint finish that is very necessary for middle distance athletes. A runner cannot shift the arms into the hard driving sprinting mode if they are already in that position. Clenched fists add to needless strain but add nothing to fluent speed.

All good runners with a poor style could be even better with an improved style. Style is at its best when the whole is even greater than the sum of the corrected parts. The fine muscle definition shown in two photographs of Seb Coe is the product of the careful speed and strength training programme necessary to achieve the good 400m pace needed for fast middle distance racing. The earlier picture, Figure 3, illustrates some still uncorrected faults of failing to relax totally at speed. The taut neck muscles and the clenched fists with spiky thumbs indicate unnecessary tension that is costly in energy and can only detract from performance.

The later photograph, Figure 4, shows the elimination of these earlier faults. The running appears effortless. If worked on carefully there are not too many faults

This sequence was taken at Crystal Palace when winning the 800m event in the McVitie meeting. In capturing the essence of the correct style for fast 800 metres racing, it reveals the powerful near sprint running style that is vital in world class middle distance racing and the 800m particularly.

Note the high knee lift of the right and leading leg and the fully straightened left and driving leg coupled to an excellent full toe-off. The high heel lift during the support phase enables a rapid follow through and the unlocking of the elbows to maximise the reaction of the arms to the powerful leg drive.

Fig 3   Seb Coe, showing tension at speed.

Fig 4   Seb Coe, showing relaxation at speed.

that cannot be eliminated or greatly reduced. Style is important, and as stated earlier, it is much more than just aesthetically pleasing.

TECHNIQUE

For the coach, technique it is the art of analysing and teaching the correct elements of the movements and the tactics of the events. For the athlete, technique is the learning, application and absorption of these elements and tactics into successful competition.

By integrating sensory information and experience with correct movement responses, a motor skill is acquired. The brain and the nervous system appear to have an unlimited capacity for acquiring new movement templates. The degree of skill achieved seems to be restricted only by physical limitations and the amount of practice.

≡5≡
THE TRAINING PROGRAMME

THE TRAINING PROGRAMME: WHAT IS ITS BASE?

An ambitious training programme requires a sound motive and a specific goal. The best motive is the pursuit of excellence and for the ambitious runner the goal is whatever major medal or title he or she values most. The route to this goal is accurately choosing the event in which the runner can reach the highest standard. This choice must not be made too early in an athlete's career. A vital part of all training is the avoidance of excess. It takes a long time to achieve the fitness, experience and confidence to compete with the best. Continued excess in any part of the training and general lifestyle will reduce, if not prematurely finish, a career in running.

The golden rule must be never to do more than is necessary to achieve a target. Never keep repeating a load that is as much as the athlete can stand. The best training programme is holistic – it allows for the development of the whole person and not just the athletic part. This is not a licence to dabble; whatever is done should be done well. Much of the time the emphasis is on the mental and physical requirements of training to reach a very high level of race fitness. Maintaining this narrow view exclusively may force many athletes into making the wrong decisions about their racing programmes and their future prospects.

To ensure success during their running careers athletes should plan to earn and maintain a decent quality of life after retirement from their sport. If they do not they become vulnerable to the desire to make as much money as they can in the short term, which usually leads to over-racing. This limits the very success they seek. The greatest success will go to those for whom excellence is more important than money.

Of course, extremes are to be avoided. An eight-hour day of heavy manual labour is not conducive to high-level athletic preparation, but not doing anything during all the hours left in the day, even after double-day training, might not be very smart. It can be boring and easily lead to staleness.

There is a prevalent notion that success is only possible if you become a full-time athlete. Not only is this demonstrably false but it is all too often a convenient excuse for not making the grade. Maybe the ultimate winners are those who can succeed in other fields when their running careers are over. But that is another story.

Any programme that involves over-racing is a bad programme. Serious racing must be treated seriously and carefully. Winter indoor races to establish mid-year training benchmarks or outings to support the club can be done without breaking training, but it would be disastrous to do this at a high level. A safe and valuable rule to follow is: *the more important the race, the higher the peaking and the longer the preparation period and tapering-off time.*

From this it is quite clear that during the main season over-racing will mean going to the line under-prepared. Either proper training time is seriously lost in all the countdown days or the athlete enters the event stale and fatigued.

SPECIFICITY

Training must be specific for maximum effectiveness. Each task has to be closely defined and for this athletes must ask themselves two questions: 'What do I want from running?' and 'Do I thoroughly understand the event?'

The first question is the more important because the answer determines the level of training the athlete must be prepared to accept, and this book is meant for the reader who is aiming high. The second requires the study of the mental and physical demands of the event by the coach and athlete so that the training can be truly specific in all areas.

Specificity is an area in which a good work physiologist can make an important contribution. After evaluating detailed tests and the degree of progress between them such an expert could, for example, advise that you need to work harder in a specific area or that you are physiologically unsuited for your chosen event.

If you have correctly chosen your event, then by regular monitoring your physiologist will be able to advise on how well you are recovering between hard sessions and where more, or perhaps less, emphasis is needed in your training. This raises a difficult problem for some coaches. Because of the difficulty of understanding much of the scientists' work they either shy away from any involvement with them or blindly follow any scientific-sounding advice from almost any source. Although the prime task of the coach is to make the athlete a better runner and not to be working for a degree in physiology, I earnestly urge coaches to try to acquire enough knowledge to enable them to evaluate at least some of the advice they may receive – if only to aid them in its application.

In a television programme on training one young athlete was asked what she had learned from all the white coats around her in the test laboratory. She replied that she had learned that the quality of the training was more important than its volume! What a waste of physiologists' time! Why had she not already been aware of this shattering glimpse of the obvious?

This is why I am always urging people to think first and then act. I based all Seb Coe's training and success on the very simple and obvious concept of 'quality first' from the very beginning. Only when all the elements of the event are recognized and understood can a training programme be constructed that will give the athlete mastery over them.

Do not forget the mental training that the physical training must provide. Physical training and mental conditioning are not in neat, separate compartments, they are interwoven into the whole fabric of the training. It is important that physical training accustoms the athlete to actual race conditions and goes even further in making the athlete become so hard that racing comes as a welcome relief. Not only should a race day feel as comfortable as a rest day, but it should also be a refreshing break from the daily grind. A careful tapering-off before big events should leave athletes composed and ready for entering the zone of optimum arousal, with no worries to affect their concentration and sharp focus on the task on hand.

Of course there will be, or should be, a certain amount of nervous tension as a safeguard against complacency. Neglecting to respect the opposition is an early step on the way to failure. If the athlete is going to compete with a driving but controlled aggression it must rest on a genuine and hard-won strength. *This cannot be obtained from wishing – only from working.*

The point is not just to develop macho runners but to produce hard competitors who are capable of winning major championships by surviving the war of attrition that all the heats, semi-finals and finals comprise. It is at the very heart of achieving a successful 800m and 1500m double when the last race, the sixth or seventh close together, may have to be the fastest of the whole series. One-off grand prix finals have featured some very great fields and produced some memorable racing, but that is not the same as Olympic pressure.

Practice may not guarantee perfection, but without a lot of rehearsing no one gets remotely near it. *The racing whole must be broken down into its constituent parts and each one practised and honed to a keen edge.*

For example, hours of practice must be devoted to transforming a simple change of pace into a sudden, startling and killing acceleration. This must be practised from different positions around the track. Later, as an added but necessary refinement, it is done with continuous all-out running for the line. These sustained high-speed runs must be done over varying distances. While some pace changes are brief, just to get into a more favourable position, some will be the final strike for home from as far as 300m out, a feat that is very difficult to sustain without fading.

Taken in 1988 during summer training in Switzerland, Peter Wirz – a 1984 Olympic 1500 metres finalist – and Seb Coe used this 1500 metres race at Rapperswill as part of their summer season build-up. Seb was just going down with a respiratory infection that was to keep him out of the 1988 Olympics.

Cross-country provides fine background training for middle distance runners, along with road racing in the early years.

Much is made of over- and under-distance work but doing some hard repetitions over the actual race distance is usually ignored. If there is no practice under equivalent race fatigue conditions then the likely result will be no sound pace judgement when the athlete is under actual and differing race conditions.

Training should frequently simulate actual racing. Under the watchful eyes of the author – as well as John Hovell, a great enthusiast and motivator – many Sunday mornings with Seb Coe at Haringey were devoted to just this. The best runners were repeating several fast, long runs while being subjected to the hurly-burly of a packed field made up from relays of fresh runners maintaining the fast pace. It was much more than hard physical conditioning: it was also developing the will-power to overcome fatigue and still accelerate to meet fresh challenges as they arise, despite the increasing distress. This is a very useful ability to have when entering the last round of a major championship. These were very demanding sessions, not easily coped with, but they did much to making racing feel easier than training – an excellent feeling for any runner to take to the start of a race!

While, at a slower pace, mileage

volume is necessary to establish a sound cardiorespiratory base, it should be limited to being just enough to achieve its aim and no more. Always limit the risk of over-use injuries. Anaerobic work is generally shorter but harder and faster. Intensity is the more powerful stimulus but if it is misused it is a quicker route to injury. Use it fully for maximum results but monitor high-intensity work very closely.

Athletes should never be pushed so hard that they break down. That is the negation of any good coaching. The harder the training, the greater the need for careful thought and sensitivity by the coach. Even so, an athlete – especially during the late junior and early senior years – must be exploring his or her limits and learning more about just how far it is possible to go. This is best done when racing against better and more experienced athletes.

LEARNING THE TRADE AND EXTENDING ONE'S LIMITS

Good opportunities for experimenting and learning for athletes at international level exist in the major county championships. All through his career, Seb Coe turned out for many county meetings in Yorkshire or Middlesex. These races had excellent fields and produced some very fast times.

In 1976 and 1977 he was learning the hard way with some very hard front running in 1500m and 1 mile races. Inevitably, he was caught during the last lap but usually, and unnoticed, a little bit later each time. Plenty of the pundits argued that he had only one way of running and he needed to learn tactics – 'front runners always lose' was the current conviction. But three of these races were at Gateshead, and it was Brendan Foster who had the foresight to say to Seb: 'Don't worry, keep going the way you are, you'll get it right in the end.' How right Brendan proved to be! He saw that Seb was simultaneously improving his staying power at speed, strengthening his will-power and extending his limits.

The following anecdote gives some insight into this aspect of the make-up of a champion. Years ago, I was walking to a training session with Seb, who was then about seventeen. I was musing, out loud, about an athlete we knew who appeared to have everything but failed to achieve. I commented that he had a good style, a good physique and so on, but somehow did not make it. Seb listened patiently and then said: 'Yes, I know Dad, but you surprise me, he's turned eighteen and never learned to hurt himself!'

≡6≡
THE PRINCIPLES OF TRAINING

Successful training depends, among other important factors, upon the coach's continuous and detailed study of the athlete. The prime purpose is to acquire as much usable data as possible that is applicable to that individual; it is important to distinguish between data and infornation. Data only becomes information if you can understand it and use it. Otherwise it is just useless clutter.

Biorhythms are a good example: even if established correctly they would in the main be unusable. The national and international race calendar is set without the promoters canvassing the potential fields to see if the dates suit their biorhythms. It is far better to study the correct application of proven physiological principles that will yield usable information than to arrive at a meeting with your resolve thoroughly undermined because the dates do not suit your biorhythms (or even your astrological signs!).

Successful middle distance racing at a high level is the specific goal. To achieve it, all the training to produce the neces-sary adaptation must also be specific. The two principles of adaptation and specificity make an excellent example of synergism: their combined effect is greater than the sum of their individual effects.

ADAPTATION

The aim of training is improvement through adaptation. Adaptation is an organism's response to repeated stimulus. Unless there is an increase in stimulus the organism will habituate (get into a rut) and there will not be any further adaptation. A neater way of saying this could be with the slogan – Progress through Progression.

In circuits, weight or interval training there are five significant variables:
- The number of repetitions in a set
- The duration of the recoveries
- The number of sets in a session
- The frequency of the sessions
- The degree of difficulty – how fast, how far or how heavy

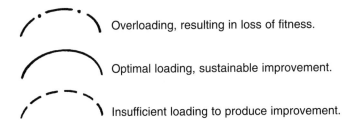

Overloading, resulting in loss of fitness.

Optimal loading, sustainable improvement.

Insufficient loading to produce improvement.

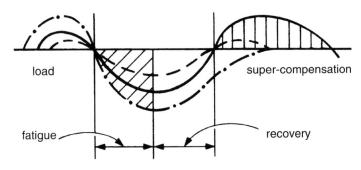

Fig 5   Diagram representing adaptation.

When used at the right time and in the right doses an increase in any one of these factors can represent progression (except recoveries, which would be shortened). As with all careful experimenting, vary only one factor at a time.

Figure 5 is a commonly used diagram derived from Yakovlev, which illustrates three basic responses to training loads. Insufficient stimulus will fail to achieve a response of super-compensation and simply produce habituation (no further gains). If the loading is excessive then the response will be a deterioration in the athlete's condition. Only if the loading is within the correct limits will the optimal amount of super-compensation occur, enhancing the athlete's fitness.

SPECIFICITY

The response to a stimulus is specific, therefore the training must be as specific as possible to each element of the event. (see Event Analysis). Inappropriate training is unnecessary stress – this can be very harmful, because high-quality distance training, particularly in middle distance work, is highly stressful anyway. An athlete must reach an equally high level of all-round fitness to cope with this heavy workload. (see Circuits and Weights).

Method

The art of training is to combine the information supplied by work physiologists with the information recorded during coaching. The former should be obtained from a regular series of tests conducted under a strict protocol in the same laboratory by the same team. Even with such a strict protocol a variation of plus or minus 3 per cent is likely; the largest part of this variation is biological variation from the athlete under test. The latter set of information comes from the coach's close and sensitive observation of the athlete under as many different conditions as possible.

This joint approach is the best. Its greatest value lies in significantly reducing the risk of subjectivity on the part of the coach. Frequent exchanges of findings will supply additional information, based on which the coach can fine tune the training towards the main goal. It is important that the coach should feed back to the laboratory all relevant performance information obtained under training and racing conditions.

When the intensity of the training is increased to obtain improved performance through further adaptation, there must be adequate provision between sessions for recovery from the increased stress. Without this proper recovery the athlete's condition will deteriorate into excessive fatigue followed by staleness. Unless this situation is promptly remedied, total breakdown will soon follow.

Ideally, the regular physiological monitoring should be accompanied by biomechanical and podiatric assessment as part of an ongoing and essential preventive maintenance programme.

There are four primary training zones to be addressed and each is defined by its physiological objective. Understanding these objectives is essential to creating the correct training schedule. Each zone will have specific distances, durations and running speeds to produce the required

Zone 1: Endurance Steady distance running at a relatively slow pace develops slow twitch (Type 1) fibres and oxidative metabolism. Better fibre recruitment giving increased efficiency. The longer the run the greater the development of muscle fuel storage. An increase in blood volume and capillaries and the development of stronger connective tissue should occur.

Zone 2: Stamina Further development of the above with some fast twitch fibres (predominantly Type 11a with possibly some Type 11b). Increased oxidative and glycolytic enzyme production and an increase in the stroke volume of the heart. (See interval training section.)

Zone 3:. This zone strongly challenges the aerobic and anaerobic abilities with the greater emphasis on the aerobic challenge accompanied by improved neurological recruitment, blood beffering capacity and further development of slow and fast twitch muscle fibres. (Type 11a and 11b.).

Zone 4: Speed plus strength This is a zone of high stress, so developing a high tolerance to the effects of acidosis is very important. This is greatly assisted by an increase in the buffering capacity of the blood. Strength and speed require the maximizing of all-round muscle fibre development together with enhanced neurological recruitment. (See Weight Training.)

Zone	Physiological adaptations	Blood lactate	Heart rate	%VO₂ max	Training interval run time	Systems challenged	Common jargon describing sessions	Training interval distance	Race pace for
4	Speed and strength ST and FT fibre development; Increased neurological recruitment; Improved blood buffering ability; Tolerance to stress of acidosis	>9mM/L; 8mM/L	200; 190	130; 100	30 sec; 2 min	Anaerobic-capacity training	Short interval; Repetitions; Short speed	200m → 1,000m	800m; 1,500m
3	Speed; ST and FT fibre development; Some increase in neurological recruitment; Some increse in blood buffering ability; Increased glycolytic enzymes	8mM/L; 7mM/L; 5mM/L	190; 180	100; 98; 90	8 min	Aerobic-capacity training	Long interval; Long speed	800m → 3,000m	3,000m; 5,000m; 1,0000m
2	Stamina; ST and some FT Type IIa development; Increased heart chamber size; Increased stroke volume; Increased oxidative/glycolytic enzymes; Increased blood volume	5mM/L; 4mM/L; 3.5mM/L	180; 160	90; 75	20 min	Anaerobic conditioning	Tempo training; Pace training; Marathon training	Marathon race pace 15–20 min	Marathon
1	Endurance; ST fibre development; Increased blood volume; Increased connective tissue development; Increased muscle fuel storage; Increased oxidative/glycolytic enzymes; Increased capillarization	3.5mM/L; 2 mM/L	160; 140	75; 60; 55	2 hr	Aerobic conditioning	Over-distance running; Base work	All longer distances	

Diagram labels: Sprint — VO₂ max — Lactate/ventilatory threshold

Table 4 Primary training zones.

adaptations. Achieving the aims of these zones depends on how well the body adapts to the training load.

The panel gives a summary of the main adaptations required in each of the four zones. Table 4 shows the increasing intensity of training but the zones are not used rigidly or only in this simple sequence.

For convenience, the four zones are laid out as quite separate divisions, but progress through them is not in neat, separate stages from the aerobic to the purely anaerobic. Throughout the year, nearly all the training sessions employed to develop the various adaptations will be in use, although in different proportions and combinations. This is how multi-pace work is used in multi-tier training.

The different sessions used on some training days might involve working in all four zones. The mix will alter as the training year progresses, so that they will all be employed in some degree throughout the training year. This becomes clearer when examining the Multi Pace training cycles.

To produce the adaptations indicated in each of these four zones, specific running sessions need to be practised diligently.

Zone 1 requires steady, over-distance runs at a relatively slow pace. Such a pace would be adequate to supply the correct physiological stimulus, but probably inadequate to condition the runner mentally for hard middle distance training and racing. Combining the two is important. The stimulus in this zone will come mainly from long and medium distance runs and the following paces are recommended.

Long runs of up to 12 miles (19km) should be at a pace of between 6:00 and 6:15 per mile (3:44/3:53 per km). Medium length runs of 6-8 miles (10–13km) at a pace of 5:30 per mile (3:25 per km). (After all, it takes running at 5:00 per mile (3:07 per km) pace to win marathons so that 5:30 per mile (3:25 per km) for shorter distances is not all that quick.)

There is a belief that trying to speed up at the end of longer runs is not wise when tired, but this is exactly what happens in races! Learn that however tired you might think you are you can *always raise a sprint at the end of any distance work.*

This was an essential element in Seb Coe's training. A good example was at the end of a hard and hilly run of 9 miles (14km) the last 400m round the end of a reservoir was run all-out. After a genuine rest as in phase 1 a good, well-trained athlete should quite easily build up to the required paces during the transition time in periodization.

In Zone 2, long and medium length runs are not abandoned, but shorter faster runs of 5 to 8km become important. These are run quickly at around 3:05 per km pace. Next, interval training is a very good method of maintaining and improving cardiac stroke and volume. Although this type of work is done using a range of intervals, it is best to separate these into sessions of long or short recoveries. To obtain the best improvement in cardiac stroke and volume the recovery must not be too short, as enough time must elapse to allow the returning copious blood flow to continue repeatedly filling the heart. This is how the chambers are strengthened and enlarged.

The increase in pace work introduced by the first type of interval training – along with circuits and weight training – starts improving neurological recruitment, blood buffering and eases the way into some faster work. The latter is important because it is always unwise to start speed work suddenly after a long period of only steady running. To avoid injury, fast twitch fibres need engaging throughout the year, getting progressively faster with time and as the weather improves.

Interval work with short or very short recoveries has a different function. This work is concerned with achieving a much higher tolerance to fast anaerobic running through an enhanced ability to buffer acidosis. This is an essential step towards using much longer intervals at fast paces when preparing for competition and is an integral part of the work in the next two zones.

Zone 3 is the long speed zone. Here long repetitions are at the heart of the training – running at or very close to Vo_2 max for up to 8 minutes is almost the equivalent of a 3000m race. By running intervals ranging from 2 to 8 minutes a good opportunity is given to learn accurate pace judgement. Also the ability to buffer is even more important if these longer repetitions are to be successfully executed. Even though acquiring long speed is the aim of the training in this zone, short fast repetitions of 200m to 400m have their place in the build-up to really fast work when getting ready for competition.

Zone 4 is the hard, repeatable 400m speed that is indispensable to top middle distance athletes and requires not just strength but the neuromuscular co-ordination of a sprinter and the high power-to-weight ratio that gives speed endurance. Of all the distance events, the 800m and 1000m races make the greatest demand for local muscular endurance at a very fast pace.

This zone involves learning to cope with high speed, very short recoveries and very high levels of acidosis. Training sessions have to be designed to condition the athlete to meet the physical attrition and the even greater mental stress encountered in major international championships. An 800m and 1500m double can require as much as six or seven hard races in only nine days.

SUMMARY OF TRAINING SESSIONS

The following strength, speed and speed endurance sessions are necessary to meet the demands of middle distance racing:
- Circuit training
- Weight training
- Plyometrics
- Sprint training – fast standing starts and short accelerations
- Long accelerations over 80 to 100m with short recoveries
- Rapid changes of pace randomly signalled at different points around the track, all off 15 second 100m speed

The following are all done from a short

rolling start that ensures an acceleration practice with each run:

- 200m to 400m runs
- Bend running practice
- 400m training – essentially long speed work, but additional short recovery work has to be used to develop sustained repeatability
- Speed endurance training, using repetitions of longer distances from 600 to 1200m

Some sessions should use the speed endurance distances in descending combinations. By progressively shortening the runs the same fast speed coupled with short rests can be maintained throughout the session.

MONITORING PROGRESS

Identify key points in the athlete's progress during the training year and set a standard for each. Some of these points will be determined by the timing of major events and some are for evaluating the athlete's physical condition. The position of these points should be indicated provisionally in the periodization table. The following are two suggested under-distance standards to be reached by first-class 800m and 1500m athletes before major competition commences:

- 200m in 22 to 22.5 seconds (ideally 21.5)
- 400m in 46 to 47 seconds

The above work is hard and very anaerobic, therefore it must be accompanied by regular distance training, which preserves a good aerobic base and maintains a high maximum oxygen uptake. It is also additional to the normal interval work.

Such comprehensive training creates a very heavy work-load. All this aerobic distance running, strength training, short and long speed work needs an early start to the training year if a smooth progression to peak performance is to be achieved. If this work is commenced early in the athlete's career it will ease the load in the senior years. Usually success goes to the forward-looking but it is foolish not to look back if it reveals something that no longer works; the history of the sport provides us with good examples of why such hard, all-round training is now so necessary.

KEEPING A TRAINING DIARY

In his book *A Scientific Approach to Distance Running* Dr David Costill makes an interesting observation:

Although measurements of muscle glycogen and blood haemoglobin concentrations may sound the alarm of over-training, the runner's sensations of effort and the stop watch are more reliable indices of staleness. The best way to determine a runner's required ratio of training to rest is to keep a training diary of mileage, intensity, performance and subjective observations.

This might not satisfy all work physiologists and coaches, because staleness is not totally a physical product. An otherwise healthy athlete may exhibit staleness

1973. After winning the English Shools 3000 metres Championship Seb Coe is seen here winning the AAA Youths 1500 metres title with a championship best performance of 3min, 55sec.

mainly, or even totally, from mental reasons. However, there is enough truth in it to heed subjective feelings and this statement adds another good reason for carefully logging training and racing.

Well kept diaries are invaluable training aids. Seb Coe's training diaries, from as far back as 1973, were a very valuable training tool. Because of ill-health 1983 was a disastrous lost year that resulted in yet more lost time in early 1984. In that year the training schedules for the run up to the Olympic 1500m were the most studied and difficult that I ever made. They incorporated five weeks of progressive training and adaptation, spaced in stages across the United States, to acclimatization to Los Angeles and an eight-hour time change. In the end a gold medal and a new Olympic record were the best endorsement of this planning. Being able to refer to the detail of those

sessions is still a great help.

This book advocates experimenting when learning the trade and later when in pursuit of excellence. Because not all experimenting, training and racing can be perfect it is essential to record anything that went amiss. This is learning from mistakes – an accurate recall of what went wrong is as important as remembering what went right.

More important than ever in global competition is recording exactly how an athlete responds to changes in the environment. How well does the runner cope with sudden media attention and how was it handled? A one-hour time change is insignificant, but two or more will be, so how long did it take to fully adjust? What plans, if any, were made to deal with the different regional and national feeding habits and how successful were they? Was the day of the race spent in the usual countdown manner? If different, why, and by how much? Was it better or worse than before? Being able to refer to all this and more is vital to successful campaigns for major international titles.

Properly kept diaries are more than an accurate record of your entire athletic career. They can provide a basis for diagnosing problems, preventing repeating mistakes, a guide to making good decisions and a protection against a faulty memory. And they only take a few minutes each day.

A properly kept diary means recording – as close as possible to the event or training session and with sufficient detail for later useful analysis – what was done, the mental and physical response at the time and simple physiological data:

What Should be Recorded

- Duration and quality of last night's sleep
- Morning heart rate before rising
- Weight – best taken before breakfast and after using the toilet
- Details and duration of all training sessions

- Weather
- Perceived exertion
- Sense of progress – comparison with previous time or conditions
- Records of all ongoing health assessments, to include even the renewal dates of shoes and orthotics

Unfortunately not all pre-printed training diaries suit everyone. Design your own layout and get a couple of months' supply photocopied, then if from experience you want to improve it you can. Do not forget that the coach should always keep a copy to compare with previously planned training schedules.

The actual layout is not vitally important, so long as it is clear and consistent. It helps when assessing improvement if the same data is always in the same place. The layout should provide for all the essentials and give adequate space to whatever is felt to need special attention.

A loose-leaf ring binder taking A4 sheets would allow for separate race and time trial results and all medical reports to be inserted. A cheap way is to use a large carbon paper triplicate book, which is then its own backup system.

≡7≡
PERIODIZATION

The next important task is to get all the elements of the training in the correct sequence and with the right emphasis. None of the foregoing will be achieved without a master plan covering short- and long-term needs. An interesting refinement in planning athletic progress is periodization.

The main advantage of developing a periodization plan is that it forces the coach and athlete to think long-term – much further ahead than just the next training session, the next week or the next race. If a carefully kept training diary is the log of the voyage then the periodization table is the navigation chart of how to get there. Comparing the second with the first provides a test of coaching and training and a good measure of how quickly the ship can get back on course after any setback.

Periodization may be described as the planned application of training stimuli to produce a specific physical condition at a particular time or place. The time might be for the major part of the competitive season or for just one major title. The place may involve planning extra time and other allowances for acclimatization.

Constructing a plan does not always require using new or fancy words. However, for clarity and the convenience of those intending further reading on this subject the technical terminology I have used follows common usage.

Basically, periodization is a system of controlled periodic loadings and recoveries. These are contained in a macrocycle. The macrocycle can be considered as a whole year (as in a single-peak cycle) or as the time from the start of the preparation period to the end of peaking or the end of the targeted major competition. The macrocycle is broken down into periods of unequal length. There are normally three periods: preparation, competition and transition.

I increase this to four, because I insist on a rest period of full recovery in the early part of the transition period. It is often correctly claimed that the transition period should not be passive. This is partly correct, because there would not be any transition with total inactivity, but it does not allow for total recovery, a vital need for athletes who train at a high level and intensity. For athletes who have had a hard year or who have performed at the highest level it is far wiser to have a period of complete rest before entering the transition phase.

Intense training utilizing fast mileage and hard anaerobic work necessitates a period of total recovery: mentally from the pressures of intense concentration, discipline and high-level competition and physically from general wear and tear and the microtraumas to the skeletal muscle. These can be shown by the presence of creatine kinase isoenzymes in blood tests taken soon after severe running or hard weight sessions. Furthermore, in the dedicated high flyer, this rest creates a renewed freshness and hunger to get out and resume training. Even so, it is not easy to get dedicated runners to give up their daily 'fix' of mileage for three or four weeks.

These four periods are in turn broken down into phases, during which there are quantitative and qualitative changes in the volume and intensity of the training. The completion of a phase marks the achievement of a specific objective inside the general training plan. A phase consists of a group of mesocycles, which usually indicate significant steps or levels of progress within the phase. Each mesocycle is made up of the microcycles necessary to achieve the immediate step-up.

Initially the time allotted to the microcycles is an arbitrary decision, which might need amending depending on the event, the wisdom of the coach and the amount of work required at each step. Genetic physiological differences between athletes endow them with differing capacities, which will show as unequal rates of development and in different areas of their training. This can affect the length and content of all the phases in a plan – as can the environment and prevailing weather conditions.

Figure 6 is a simplified diagram of a single-week microcycle showing successive and safe loading to produce increasing adaptation. Note that the seventh day is a rest day. If the period between training sessions is not excessive, no deterioration of fitness will occur and the athlete will start the next session stronger and refreshed. In the United States, programming is centred around the rather short collegiate season, which may account for the lengths of their mesocycles being around three or four weeks and a microcycle one week. Most European countries – with longer seasons and less climatic contrasts – tend to use longer cycles, often twice these lengths.

These differences between athletes are sufficient to make it unwise to generalize about the number of units in a single training session. Each coach will have to decide the volume of work that makes up a unit for each type of training. If, for a distance runner, a day's training session is 12 miles (19km) of steady running then what distance at what pace constitutes a unit? And how many short recovery fast 200m repetitions are there in this type of session?

Some might consider that just one type of run represents a single unit. If, for instance, a 8 miles (13km) run counted as one unit and was performed daily, then with one rest day this allows for six units of work per week. Athletes on a more

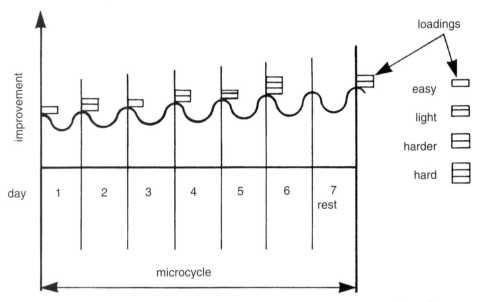

Fig 6 *Diagram of single week microcycle. The loadings shown indicate a commonly used hard/easy sequence.*

intensive programme will use double-day training and every extra session, plus any sets stimulating different zones, would represent an extra unit in the microcycle. Thus an athlete doing double-day training on Tuesdays, Thursdays and Saturdays would complete a minimum of nine units per week.

A set of four 1600m runs or six to eight 800m runs is one unit, but if another session were to contain a set of specific speed drills as well as some fast repetitions over 200 or 300m this would count as two units. Circuits and weights are more units to be included.

When building up to a peak, a top-class international athlete might in the course of a double-day workout perform the following. In the morning, a brisk 3 to 5 mile (5–8km) run, a recovery while resting and changing shoes, then a set of six or eight hard, short-recovery 300m intervals. In the afternoon, a 6 miles (10km) fartlek (a variable pace run) on undulating park land.

The contents of these microcycles are the fine tuning of the training. It is easy to see that in compiling too much fine detail you can lose sight of the need to have a flexible approach.

The following is a summary of some of the principal units to be considered when constructing the microcycles and mesocycles used in the build-up of a middle distance macrocycle:

- Aerobic and anaerobic conditioning runs
- Aerobic and anaerobic capacity runs

75

- Strength and stamina work on long and short hills
- Regular and controlled fartlek
- Interval training
- Fast bend running
- Specific speed drills
- Repeatable all-out 400m pace work
- Pace change rehearsals
- Circuit and weight training

PEAKING

When the physical condition aimed for is maximal it is called a peak. Whether one or two peaks are required depends upon the runner's aspirations, which might be for both winter and summer major performances or one supreme effort.

It is my very firm belief that athletes who want to be the best must have enough conviction to put all their eggs in one basket and decide just where their ultimate goal lies. Once this decision is made they must work single-mindedly for that chosen goal to the athletic exclusion of any other. For this reason I have always considered that when going for the big prize – one that is commensurate with the athlete's current level of development – the highest and most effective peak is reached once and only once in a year.

Whether aiming for a national youth title at one end of the scale or an Olympic championship at the other, it is the professional, single-minded approach that is the most successful. The diagrams and tables I have used to illustrate periodizing are those of single-peaking. Those who wish to double-peak will have care-

fully to assess different rates of build-up to their events.

The above comments do not imply that athletes may not compete during their off-season. The judicious use of cross-country and road running has an important role in the overall development – as does indoor competition – as long as the results obtained are for progress assessment only and are not specifically targeted and trained for. Anything more than a reasonable rest for one or two days beforehand will limit the accuracy of the evaluation. The best use of such competition is to provide a better assessment of the athlete's current condition and the coach's work to date, enabling them to fine tune their training schedules.

One winter, in one of our usual indoor 3000m assessment races, Seb was only placed third. It took only two weeks to adjust the endurance factor and win over the same distance in a high-class field. An added advantage is that a little competition can make a welcome and refreshing change for the athlete.

Elsewhere in this book great emphasis is placed on planning, particularly long-term planning. Periodization, which can be so highly detailed, is a good example but it must be pointed out that such closely planned scheduling has its pitfalls. Any practical coach knows that even one season – never mind a year or a career – is a long period for an athlete to survive without any setbacks of either long or short duration, be they infections or injuries.

FLEXIBILITY IN PLANNING

The modern coach needs to exercise management skills. One of the yardsticks of good management is the speed with which an athlete can get back on course after being diverted from the planned path. All planning must therefore be flexible. While containing enough detailed information to indicate the correct training emphasis and its timing, a periodization table will always be the best reference as to where the athlete's progress should be.

Many of the periodization tables that appear from around the world are over-detailed. They present a great risk of locking an athlete into a training routine that for various reasons – such as sickness, staleness, fatigue, work or examinations – may have become inappropriate and if pursued would only make matters worse.

Field events, sprints and hurdles have a larger technical content, which permits a more detailed analysis for periodization, but it is just as easy to be knocked off course by the greater risk of traumatic injuries from many of the training elements in throwing and jumping. In distance running the training stresses are applied continuously for much longer units of time. This alone is enough to cause a variety of over-use injuries.

Circumstances often dictate that many athletes must work more remotely from their coaches than they would prefer, and cannot have frequent personal supervision. Therefore there might be a strong desire to give a detailed training schedule covering a fairly long period and this can easily create a communication problem which must be overcome. Equally, it is not an excuse for not developing a plan. The key to any successful programme is providing enough time at the right moment for adequate recovery and discussion.

Table 5 represents a sample single-peak periodization for an athlete aiming at one major event, title or record. The training year starts carefully and then progresses to a more intense build-up. Note the total rest of three or four weeks

Period	Rest	Transition	Preparation		Competition Early Late	
Phase	Mid Sep 1	Mid Oct–Nov 2	Dec–Apr 3	May 4	Jun–Jul 5	Aug–Mid Sep 6 Peaking
Week	0 4	5 11	32	37	45	52

Table 5   Periodization – phase table for single-peaking.

Period	Weeks	Aerobic conditioning	Lactate/ ventilatory threshold	Aerobic capacity training	Anaerobic capacity training	Total running units	Total miles	Mobility	Strength	Total units
Phase 1	4	–	–	0	–	0	–	–	–	–
Transition Phase 2	4	4	1	0	0	5	30–35	3	2	10
	4	4	1	1	0	6	35–40	4	2	12
Preparation	2	4–5	1–2	1	1	7–9	45–50	4	2	13–15
	3	4–5	2	2	1	9–10	50–55	4	2	15–16
Phase 3	4	5–6	3	2	1	11–12	55–60	4	3	18–19
	4	4–5	4	2	1	11–12	60–65	5	2	18–19
	4	4–5	4	2	2	12–13	60–65	5	2	19–20
	4	4	5	2	2	13	65–70	4	2	19
Pre-Competition Phase 4	5	4–5	5	3	2	14–15	70–75	4	2	20–21
Early Competition Phase 5	4	4	5	2	3	14	65–70	4	1	19
	4	3	5	2	3	13	55–60	4	1	18
Main Competition and Peaking Phase 6	2	3	4	3	3	13	50–55	4	1	18
	2	3	3	4	4	14	50	4	1	19
	2	2	2	2	4	10	40	4	0–1	16–17

See Table 1 for examples of the strength units in this table.

Table 6   Periodization – example of a table for one year.

in phase 1 prior to the transition phase. It is suitable for middle distance athletes, including 5000m runners, for whom the main target for their year is a major championship or perhaps one or two of the more prestigious grand prix meetings that take place between August and mid September. If the main objective is a major indoor or cross-country championship, the peak is moved up the periodization calendar to the relevant time.

For those who insist on double-peaking to achieve both aims it is most likely that the end result will be a diminished performance in one, if not both. This is because double-peaking effectively halves the available preparation time for each peak – unduly forcing progress and probably limiting the quality of the peak. Moreover, double-peaking makes it difficult, if not impossible, to give athletes in long and very hard training the complete rest breaks that serious competitors need.

Table 6 shows a periodization layout for a whole year, but it might not always be appropriate to have a very detailed sheet specifying the exact contents of each macrocycle. Once the target for each phase has been selected the coach can evaluate the athlete's progress and select suitable sessions for the microcycles. If the rate of progress differs from the expected the coach might, for example, think that a set of 800m is preferable to the set of 600m originally planned; a fixed script might be unhelpful. Also, if the athlete has a copy of all or part of the overall periodizing table the coach runs the risk of the athlete observing the variations and wondering if the coach is sure of

what he or she is doing. It is always risky to give a lengthy schedule to an athlete who is way from the coach for long periods and is coached by post.

Starting with the long rest in Phase 1, resist any urge to indulge in a strenuous game of soccer or tennis because of a surge of renewed energy. While a non-load bearing exercise such as swimming is fine, do it in moderation. Do not let your natural competitiveness spill over into making a game of tennis into a Wimbledon final. Light callisthenics and your usual flexibility routine are all that is necessary to keep you ticking over safely. The goal at this stage is to relax from the stress of hard training and competition and emerge fresh and eager for the coming season.

Phase 2 is the transition back to training. This involves gently resuming the various elements of training, with the emphasis falling on easy distance running. There is also a gentle reintroduction of light circuit training as a prelude to starting weight training again. But the main aim is to recover any slight loss of cardiopulmonary conditioning that may have occurred. Happily, any such loss is rapidly restored. With the judicious use of a few light speed drills of short duration an athlete is soon back into full training.

Phase 3 is important. At all distances speed is vital, and if speed is the name of the game never get too far away from it. Because speed carries with it a greater risk of injury it requires a long and very careful programme of development. Far too many injuries are the result of sudden changes, be they shoes or drastic changes in training. Therefore this is the time to introduce elements of faster work carefully. Middle distance racing calls for sustained high speed and *as speed is the name of the game then never get too far away from it in training.*

Phase 4 is the pre-competition phase. Now is the time for the coach and athlete to review their winter progress. If they have been using any winter competitions for evaluation purposes (without departing from normal training) the review will reveal the areas that most need extra attention. This is when adjustment by fine tuning the microcycles is the key to further progress.

Towards the end of this phase it may be opportune to compete in county championships or support your club in a good-class league meeting to regain familiarity with competition – especially if there has been no winter indoor competition. As an exception to avoiding competing and training for a major title outside the summer season, it sometimes can be beneficial to expose the exceptionally promising junior or young senior athlete to international competition in meetings such as the European Indoor Championships.

By Phase 5 the coach and athlete should have selected the meetings and events in which the athlete will be competing. As in the latter part of phase 4, the microcycle might now require adjustment almost on a daily basis, although it may be difficult for the coach and athlete to achieve such frequent contact. Planning the minimum number of races of progressive difficulty to achieve maximum performance will allow the most

time for training and recovery, which helps to avoid staleness and injuries. To ensure a good performance in meaningful events the athlete must taper off before racing. As this diminishes the time available for training, it follows that an athlete with a heavy racing programme has diminished his of her chances of good performances.

Towards the end of this phase a reduction begins in the heavier weight training programme of 800m and 1500m runners, but good strength must be maintained. Until now, part of the programme will have been a steady build-up of distance work to enhance endurance and stamina. Utilizing aerobic and anaerobic conditioning paces, maximum distance should be reached around the middle of May and maintained for about three weeks, finishing at the end of the first week of June.

From now until the end of June the emphasis falls on both long and short speed endurance. This aerobic and anaerobic capacity work is extremely demanding. It necessitates a significant reduction in weekly distance and very careful planning to balance the hard anaerobic work with the strength and conditioning units. The remainder of this phase will have to cater for the more serious build-up events leading to the peak during Phase 6. Continuing care must be taken to ensure adequate recovery from these hard sessions.

Phase 6 is the second phase of competition. Any racing at this time is even more carefully selected and is only to sharpen the athlete. It will include the principal goal for the athlete's year. By now the cumulative stress of training and competition renders many high performing athletes more vulnerable to debilitating and often serious viral or even parasitic infections – hence the continual warning notes about proper recovery. Medical evidence is mounting to show that the cells of athletes in hard training are more permeable to invasion than those of less active people.

Against a background of a considerably reduced mileage, special attention is given to maintaining and even further developing sustainable speed. The training should include units of short, fast repetitions with matching short recoveries. Sessions devoted to bend running and rapid changes of pace from various positions around the track and sustained over varying distances are important.

A peaking phase must be considered as a failure if it does not leave the athlete mentally and physically sharp, confident and eager to compete. At the end of a hard year of training and racing a return to Phase 1 should be welcomed and very good use made of it.

≡8≡
MULTI-PACE AND MULTI-TIER TRAINING

While it is true that there have been a few successful 400/800m types at the top level, they were not true middle distance runners. The best, and this is significant, have always had the ability to perform well over a wide range of distances, because they are endurance-based but possess good speed. Seb Coe was good from 400m to 3000m and ran well in cross-country and road relays. Saïd Aouita broke records from 1 mile to 5000m and Steve Ovett's ability ranged from 800m to the half-marathon. Likewise, David Moorcroft and Ian Stewart were class 1500m and 5000m runners. It cannot be stressed too often that while successful middle distance racing requires good 400m speed it is still an endurance-based event.

MULTI-PACE TRAINING

A good case can be made for using fast 5000m training as the best base upon which to build in early spring. Multi-pace training sessions are biased towards this longer distance during this period.

Multi-pace training has its origin in a pertinent observation made some years ago by Frank Horwill, the founder of the British Milers Club. At that time middle distance training was studied less than it is now and the training methods gave rise to an anomaly that he spotted. The best times for the half-mile were those of the quarter-milers who had moved up an event and the best mile times were those of the three milers who had come down in distance. From this it was a short step to appreciating that the half-milers were not fast enough and the milers lacked stamina. (Unfortunately, logic does not always prevail and some odd ideas arose. Now we see the very opposite situation in which 400m runners who are not good enough for the top spot at their original distance move up to 800m without the requisite endurance background – particularly in speed endurance. Although sometimes called an extended sprint,

82

modern 800m racing is too long and far too fast at the top level for this move to be successful.)

To remedy the situation, Frank Horwill saw that a training method was needed that would best combine speed with endurance. To meet this need he devised multi-pace training. For me the appeal was instantaneous as it crystallized some of the ideas I had already formed. It is logical and the best system I know. I believe in the concept totally and I have practised it very successfully for a long time. As with any coaching system or method, it must be used sensitively.

It is not a formula or a simple recipe for instant success; it is the basis for a comprehensive training system that must be applied imaginatively and with each session tailored to suit the individual athlete. Sessions suitable for a world-class male 800m runner – although similar in principle – are not suitable for a female 3000m athlete, no matter how good she might be.

The principle on which this training is based is that the athlete should train at four or five different combinations of paces and distances in a multi-pace cycle. The duration of a cycle may be varied during the training year to accommodate periods of higher distance or any extra emphasis felt to be needed at the time. An average cycle is about ten to fourteen days.

MULTI-TIER TRAINING

To maximize the benefits of this system it has to be integrated into the periodiza-

tion: a plan of steady development throughout the training year towards a peak. I call this multi-tier training because after one or two cycles the paces or the recoveries (or both) will be adjusted to produce higher levels of adaptation.

Each tier has the same layout: similar work is done as in the equivalent tier below but usually at a higher intensity or changed volume. Layer upon layer of increasing fitness is built up until peaking is achieved.

Table 7 shows a suggested 12-day cycle suitable for a middle distance runner. As explained earlier, the speeds of the runs and the durations of the recoveries will vary as the athlete progresses. It is an example of multi-pace training using five different paces during the 12-day cycle. The paces are those of the athlete's best times for the pace distance: if the best time for the 800m is 1:52 then the time for each 400m run of the 800m pace session is 56 seconds. If the best 800m time were 1:42 the time for each 400m would be 51 seconds.

In the transition phase these runs might be a little slower, reflecting the runner's current level of fitness. Later in the year when peaking, the times for the runs of 800m or less may be much quicker. Also, during the second half of Phase 3 and the first week of Phase 4, a steady build-up to high distance is required. During this period it is quite acceptable to substitute harder and longer runs for some or all of the fartlek sessions.

Again, as in periodization, do not get locked into a completely rigid multi-pace programme. For example, if later in the year it was considered that more speed was needed in the 5000m pace speed endurance session, it would be perfectly acceptable occasionally to substitute another session that would be faster but equally demanding of stamina. Such a session might be the old Haringey favourite of a medley of distances, where in repeat runs varying from 1200m down to 400m the speed is stepped up but combined with enough distance to ensure stamina. Multi-pace training is an excellent system, but use it flexibly. It is not something to get locked into with endless repetition so the athletes know the day of the week by the sessions they run!

Table 7 does not show any double-day training that may need to be incorporated

into the extra training modalities of special sessions and those of total physical conditioning into the full cycle. Only the different training paces that are at the heart of this method are shown.

Some athletes may find a 14-day cycle much better. I have, for example, trained athletes for whom a regular Saturday rest day was more suited to meeting their other commitments. Such a programme could be as shown in Table 8.

The 12-day and 14-day multi-pace cycles shown are not complete training schedules for the periods given. What they show are the essential elements or paces that have to be worked on. Additional to these suggested schedules is all the other necessary work to make the

	Day	Session	Pace
1	Sun	4 × 1500m or 3 × 2000m	5000m
2	Mon	Fartlek	
3	Tues	8 × 800m	3000m
4	Wed	Road run	
5	Thurs	16 × 200m	1500/mile
6	Fri	Rest if racing, if not Fartlek	
7	Sat	Race or time trial	
8	Sun	4–6 × 400m	800m
9	Mon	Road run	
10	Tues	2 × 300m, 4 × 200m, 4 × 100m	400m
11	Wed	Fartlek	
12	Thurs	Time trial or race, or choose a suitable training pace for the next event, e.g. 400m pace for an 800m race, 800m pace for a 1500m race, or 1500m pace for a 5000m race.	

Table 7   Multi-pace training, 12-day cycle.

	Day	Session	Pace
1	Sun	4 × 4 min	5000m
2	Mon	Fartlek	
3	Tues	8 × 800m	3000m
4	Wed	Road race	
5	Thurs	16 × 200m	1500m
6	Fri	Fartlek	
7	Sat	Rest	
8	Sun	4–6 × 400m	800m
9	Mon	Road run	
10	Tues	4 × 300m, 4 × 200m,	400m
11	Wed	Fartlek	
12	Thurs	1000m + 800m + 600m + 400m	1500m
13	Fri	Easy road run	
14	Sat	Rest day, perhaps 1500m race on Sunday	

Table 8 Multi-pace training, 14-day cycle.

complete racer, including sessions of stamina-maintaining mileage, strength training, general conditioning, special speed and acceleration runs. By the end of Phase 3 all this work will become faster and harder. This makes for a very demanding and tiring training programme.

To allow for adequate recoveries from this intensive training, one rest day or week is built into the schedule. No doubt those who are hooked on high mileage or massive volumes of low-intensity work will see only an extra 52 lost training days in addition to the end of season lay-off that very few take yet is so essential. Always remember that under-recovery is effectively over-training and that excessive distance running at any pace will end in injury. Success at the top level in modern middle distance racing requires a lot of very hard and intensive speed and

speed endurance work. Without an adequate maintenance programme using great care and proper recoveries, breakdown will occur even quicker.

The 14-day multi-pace cycle with its regular Saturday rest day may appear to be the rigid same-thing-on-the-same-day sort of programme that is to be avoided. In practice this need not be true. It does contain the strongly recommended weekly rest day, but it also indicates that sessions differing from those in the 12-day multi-pace cycle can be used to practise running at any particular pace. Physically and mentally this provides a better training practice as it covers the five different paces with greater variety and flexibility. It also makes it easier to progress to the next level or tier in the multi-tier build-up when approaching peaking.

In this system the athlete does not com-

Distance	Formula	Example
5000m	3X + 159 sec	13 min 19 sec
3000m	2X + 36 sec	7 min 56 sec
1500m	X sec	3 min 40 sec
800m	½X − 2 sec	1 min 48 sec
400m	¼X− 6.5 sec	48.5 sec

Table 9   Table for calculating equivalent race times.

mence the repetitions in the tables by basing the paces on personal best times. The times are adjusted upwards to provide and match the athlete's progress. Also, when using single peaking, nothing needs to be rushed. The whole concept is that all areas of speed and speed endurance are developed gradually and simultaneously until peaking commences.

At this stage, we are attempting to do two things. If balance has been achieved then the task is to maintain it, but if one special aspect of racing readiness needs special attention to enhance it, this must be done without losing the general balance. This is at the heart of successful fine tuning.

Never forget the reason for the road runs and fartlek. Their purpose is to improve racing, so never let the pace slacken unduly. This easily happens between accelerations in fartlek, so always kick off at a good pace and not in spurts that are too short. *Would-be champions cannot afford too much slow road miles or go-as-you-please.*

I strongly believe that the all-round accomplished middle distance athlete must be able to produce fast times in at least one event above and below his or her chosen distance. This is the minimum acceptable range for a well-trained runner. Saïd Aouita, Steve Ovett, Steve Cram and Seb Coe could all do it, and Table 9 gives the calculations for the times that should be achieved, using the 1500m time X as the base for a male runner. This 1500m time of 3 minutes 40 seconds is chosen as a reminder to a young but improving male athlete that any significant progress that he hopes to make will depend on meeting at least the 800m and 3000m times, and that anything better will require even better 400m speed. This underlines the value of multi-pace training sessions.

The table will be very useful to runners who might be unsure how to choose the correct training pace, say, for a 400m or 5000m pace if they have no actual times for these events. These formulae will supply a suitable estimated event time from which the pace for the season can be calculated. (For female runners substitute their own best time for X and make the appropriate calculations.)

=9=

TRAINING SESSIONS

When commencing interval training the following method is recommended to establish the initial paces for the interval that is chosen. (The 'interval' always refers to the run and not the recovery.)

To the runner's best time for the distance run add 25 per cent. Progress by reducing the percentage allowance in 5 per cent steps. This automatically shortens the recovery time if the work–relief ratio is maintained as shown in Table 10.

The reason why the table shows the duration of the run rather than the distance is because in this form it is easier to apply to various levels of fitness or abiliy. When approaching peak condition the pace at which the intervals are run is one that just permits the session to be completed with the allowed recovery. Once the athlete and coach are satisfied that the maximum speed that can be maintained for a set has been achieved, the recovery time is shortened still further.

A favourite session of Seb Coe was running six to eight 300m runs with all the intervals around 36 to 38 seconds – with one or two at around 35 or even 34 seconds – and the recovery not exceeding 45 seconds. He considered this to be his acid test of readiness for major competition, to be reached before the correct tapering-off period commenced to allow major events and titles to be run when fully recovered and fresh.

A basic introductory interval session for middle distance and 5000m runners is working up the number of 200m repetitions. A good 1500m runner should be able to manage a session of thirty 200m runs each in 30 seconds with 1 minute recoveries without feeling distressed. An athlete contemplating a 5000m run in around 13:12 will have to put in a lot of 63 second and even 62 second laps to achieve this time, so the ability to run a set of thirty 200m runs at 30 second pace is really not so demanding.

Some coaches employ 'up the clock' sessions, but I have modified these to include sessions in which there is an increase in speed with the increase in distance. Once this type of run has been mastered, the next and hardest step is to run as above but with a diminishing recovery. This is not so extraordinary because this is a logical progression towards racing conditions.

The sessions using fast short distance

Energy System	Interval Time	Work/Relief Ratio	Type of Relief
ATP-CP-(LA)*	10 sec		Walking and/or
	15 sec	1:3	flexing
Short Speed	20 sec		
(All Out)	25 sec		Walking

* Sometimes erroneously called an 'alactic' zone although there isn't any totally alactic running. However in short sprints LA is not a greatly inhibiting factor for well-trained endurance middle distance runners.

Energy System	Interval Time	Work/Relief Ratio	Type of Relief
ATP-CP-LA	30 sec	1:3	Light to mild
Long speed	40–50 sec		exercise
95-100%	1:00-1:10 sec		
All Out	1:20 sec	1:2	Jogging
LA-O_2	1:30-2:00 min	1:2	Work relief
95% All Out	12:10-2:40 sec		
Speed+			
Endurance	2:50-3:00 min	1:1	Rest relief
O_2	3:00-4:00 min	1:1	
Endurance			Rest relief
90% All Out	4:00-5:00 min	0.5:1	

Table 10   Interval training – a guide to recoveries.

intervals followed by adequate recoveries have as their main function the development of the adenosine triphosphate and creatine phosphate system to increase energy storage. Another use is to develop the ability to cope with repeated high speeds. This can be achieved by running 100m repetitions with very short recoveries. Often called 'back to back' running, these repetitions are performed at a very fast pace with a jogged return. Top-class athletes will even do them with no more than a cautious slowing up and a quick turn round. Such sessions are only for those who have become slowly and very carefully accustomed to this type of workload. It is virtually a form of continuous sprinting – it is very tiring and injury prone if not performed carefully.

The variations and combinations of different runs or intervals are almost infinite. This gives the vigilant and observant coach plenty of opportunities to address and remedy any weakness or deficiencies in training as it progresses. It must not be assumed that all interval work consists of repeating the same distance in every run, the 'up the clock' and 'down the clock' sessions are as much part of interval training as are the more common sessions of twenty or thirty 200m runs.

The advantage of 'down the clock' runs lies in the fact that a very fast pace might be set on the first run, and maintained even with the comparatively short recoveries accompanying the diminishing distances run. This session has an additional advantage. Not only does it allow for maintaining a fast pace, but by relaxing the recoveries slightly it permits the coach and athlete to use faster speeds for the initial longer intervals than is otherwise possible. A very useful session is provided by the following: one 1200m run, two 800m runs, one 600m run, and one or two 400m runs. No hard and fast rules are possible for the recoveries, as these will depend so much upon the status of the athlete. When he or she is fully fit and well into the hard training the recoveries should be only just long enough to permit the athlete to complete the assigned sessions. At other times the recoveries outlined in Table 10 are a good guide, particularly when the athlete starts this type of session for the first time.

Suitable surfaces and gradients may be exploited in interval training sessions and at the same time may give the additional stimulus that hill running can provide. The training session that progressively works up to thirty or forty 100m runs up a 1-in-6 gradient provides just such a good example (see Figure 11 later in this chapter).

CONTROLLED OR PSEUDO FARTLEK

This is a session that produces a very

powerful stimulus and should be used and monitored with great care. It is best conducted with athletes who are very closely matched in all-round ability and it is quite unsuitable for large, disparate groups.

Select a suitable circuit, which should be about 400m and must contain a short hill of around 80 to 100m. Thus the coach has downhill, uphill and flat running on the same circuit. A sound choice of surface would be good grass, say in a public park. The great advantage of this session is that unlike regular fartlek, in which athletes run faster or slower of their own volition, the runners have to respond to an outside signal. This is much closer to actual racing conditions when, no longer able to go as they please, they have to respond to repeated surges by other competitors and not when they feel like it. It is referred to as controlled (or 'pseudo') fartlek.

The athletes are instructed that on hearing a blast from a whistle they are to sprint as hard as they can until signalled to stop by a further blast. The duration of the run and whether or not it is level, uphill or downhill sprinting is entirely at the discretion of the coach. This mandates two things. First, acute observation by the coach, which is easier if he or she has a good knowledge of the athletes. Second, good self-control by the coach – it is important not to be too ambitious and to exercise proper restraint. While such a session can be made to last up to 30 minutes it is possible to exhaust even the fittest athlete in less than 10 minutes!

This is why it is inadvisable to try and

work with a group of widely varying abilities. Some will be left behind and be running downhill while others are working on the flat or uphill and all control of the session is lost. Some will be prematurely exhausted while others are still fresh. Ideally it is better to use a small group of four or five runners of closely matched abilities. It is better still, although rare, if they are all in the same event. This can offer a good opportunity to compare strengths and weaknesses in each runner as guides to adjusting their individual programmes.

SPECIAL SESSIONS

Training must be holistic. To satisfy this condition fully the physical training must be such that it significantly contributes to conditioning the mind to the rigours of racing. This enables the athlete to go

---

Stage 1 This set is made up of eleven runs progressing in 10m steps between 100m and 200m (Figure 7). In all these sets the time added to each successive interval in a set is always the same, so the pace increases with each run. This first example begins with a run at a 1500m pace of 3:45, taking 15 seconds, and finishes with a run at a 400m pace of 47 seconds, taking 23.5 seconds. The additional time to be added to each run is obtained by dividing the difference between the last and the first target times by the number of steps and the calculation is as follows. The eleven runs require ten steps or increases. The difference between the first run and the last is 8.5 seconds. Dividing this figure by 10 gives 0.85 seconds, the time to be added to each successive run. The total distance run at speed is 1650m.

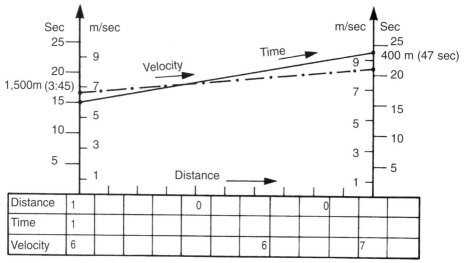

Fig 7   Increasing speed with increasing distance.

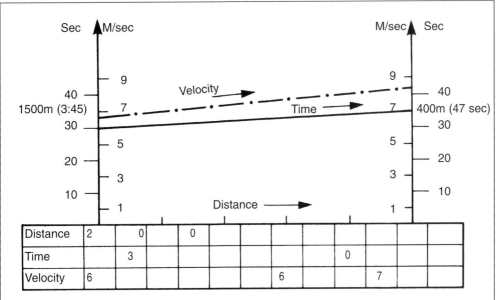

	Sec	M/sec						M/sec	Sec	
Distance	2		0		0					
Time			3					0		
Velocity	6						6		7	

Fig 8   As Figure 7, but using longer distances.

Stage 2   In this stage the lengths of the intervals range from 200m to 300m in 20m steps using the same starting and finishing paces. This time there are only six runs, which gives five steps of 1.05 seconds each and the recoveries are easy jogs back over the same distance as the run. The total distance run at speed is 1500m (Figure 8).

Stage 3   The difference between this stage and Stage 2 is in the recoveries. Instead of a jog back over the same distance as the run, the recoveries shorten in the following way. At the completion of each fast interval the runner continues on round the track in a slow jog back to the start. In this way the athlete not only runs farther and faster each time but does it with the recoveries diminishing from 200m down to 50m. Now the athlete is beginning to get closer to continuous running with increasing speed.

beyond what he or she thought was their limit when the need arises. To this end, here are five very useful progressive sets that simultaneously increase speed and distance. These will help to develop the ability to increase the pace steadily during a race and finish with a fast last lap, as in the 1500m and miling.

In all these sets the middle distance runner is acquiring the ability and the confidence that he or she can, within the distance of the event, run faster the farther the distance. The method employed is to commence the first interval at 1500m pace and finish the last one at 400m pace. When practising Stage 1 the recoveries are the same distance as the intervals and the runner soon progresses from walking to

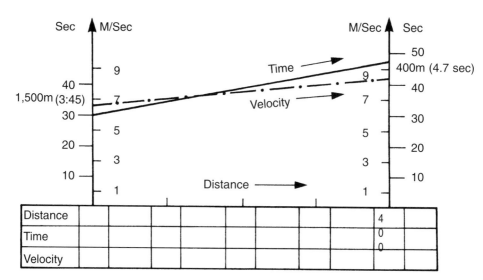

Fig 9   As Figure 8, but more severe.

Stage 4   This set has the same start and finish paces as the other sets, but has the fewest and the longest intervals. They range from 200m to 400m in four 50m steps, each having a time increase of 4.25 seconds. The recoveries are a slow jog back over the same distance as the run. Although the total distance run at speed in all these stages is similar, increasing the length of the intervals makes the sets much harder although there are fewer in each set (Figure 9).

Stage 5   As in Stage 3, after each interval the athlete continues on round the track to the start, thus reducing the recoveries so that the last one is only 50m to the start of the final run. The set of five runs requires four steps. Subtracting the 200m time of 30 seconds from the 400m time of 47 seconds gives 17 seconds, a time increase of 4.25 seconds for each run. There is another advantage attached to mastering these sessions – the athlete will have acquired a feeling for accurate pace judgement over a wide range of middle distance racing speeds.

jogging back to the start. From Stage 2 onwards all the sets are run with jogged recoveries. All intervals commence with a short rolling start.

Short sprints make an effective speed drill, as shown in Figure 10. As it involves

rapid changes of direction it not only enhances the ability to change pace but also develops agility. This session can be performed with a jog-back recovery or, with practice, with a fast return run. For the very fit, a continuous set of four runs

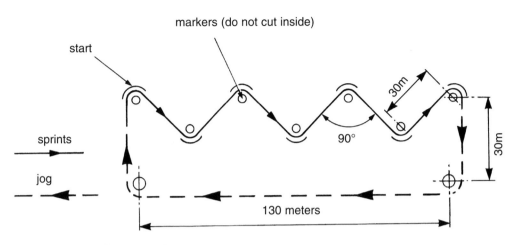

markers (do not cut inside)

start

sprints

jog

90°

30m

30m

130 meters

Fig 10   Short acceleration session.

can be done as part of a speed endurance session, mixing in accelerations while maintaining a good pace. The total distance of this repeat set is approximately 1500m, which can make a good contribution to a hard speed endurance workout.

While this might be familiar to some soccer players in one form or another it must be treated carefully by highly trained runners, especially when tried out for the first time. The risk comes from the repeated braking to negotiate each marker and the placing of strong rotational forces on the knees and ankles.

SPRINTING

Sprinting is high speed plus rapid acceleration, which is very different from simply running quickly. Although I have stressed that the 800m and 1500m races are endurance-based events, I have equally emphasized the need to develop all-out speed coupled with rapid acceleration. As well as the tactical advantage it brings, developing a powerful sprint has another very important use. The higher the maximum pace becomes, the higher is the athlete's sustainable sub-maximum speed.

A middle distance racer should ensure that his or her arm carriage is not too high. In order to sprint the arm action must change from one that should be easy, smooth and economic to one of vigour, power and drive. If the arms are already being carried too high they cannot change to the sprinting mode. They must do this to increase their share of the reaction to the increased drive from the legs, another good reason for middle distance runners to enhance upper body development. For this to happen the upper arm must be drawn well back and high up, simultaneously unlocking the elbow before it is brought forward forcibly with the hand and wrist loose but controlled.

93

Taken at an indoor meet at Cosford this is an excellent example of relaxed bend running. Mastering fast bend running is a great asset in 800 metres racing and is essential to success on a 200 metres track. It could be crucial on the last bend in a very fast 200 metres of a very slow 1500 metres event, which could be run in 24 sec or even better.

A sprinter should keep the elbows close to the sides, with the forearms parallel and the arms restricted to a fore and aft movement without passing across the chest. When running, even briskly, it is possible for the trunk to contra-rotate slightly at each stride to contribute to the reaction to the driving leg. But when moving at 4 to 5 strides per second the shoulders remain steady and it is impossible for the trunk to respond that quickly, therefore much more is demanded from the arms. At sub-maximum pace a smooth, economical running style is very important – but when running all-out the dominant need is for a much higher knee lift, a straightened out driving leg and very flexible ankle for maximum toe-off. The lower heel flick used when running at sub-maximum pace changes to a very high one when running all-out. The follow-through leg should fold up completely to let the heel almost touch the buttock, bringing the centre of gravity of the leg closer to the hip joint. This permits a much faster rotation about the hip joint and with it a quicker stride rate or cadence. All these factors will need special strength and flexibility attention.

The foot-plant is different in sprinters. They are more up on their toes and their heels hardly kiss the ground. At some stage of a sprint acceleration, even in a race, there will be a more forward body lean, at least until maximum speed is achieved.

Sprinting in any form, whether as a rapid change of pace for position in a race, a very fast start to an 800m event or a fast finish to a slow mile, has its own skills. These skills have to be slowly and carefully learned and practised until they can be performed well when required and when under pressure. The ability to sprint must be available at any moment in a race, so it might commence anywhere around the track. Even when practised with a rolling start, the time for a 100m stretch will be affected by where it is started on the track. An allowance for this should be made if any of the repeat runs are timed.

Despite the influence of a runner's genetic make-up, sprinters are made, not born. This ability does not come naturally; it will need a lot of hard work. Furthermore, fierce as sprinting can be, the best do it with the maximum possible relaxation, which also requires a lot of practice.

Although this section is titled Special Sessions, this is not a sprint training programme, nor is it an example of sprint training sessions; it is to emphasize that sprinting requires very special attention if significant improvement is to be made. Coaches, and athletes who want to improve their sprinting, should read specific sprint literature to help them build the right schedule for them, always remembering that it must fit in with speed endurance because the 800m and 1500m are endurance events.

HILL RUNNING

Correct hill running, regularly practised, should be a very important part of the training of any middle distance athlete. Whereas some live in areas where hills

Type 1 These are the fairly gentle hills found on an undulating road or not too severe British cross-country courses during distance training. They challenge the athlete's ability to change pace or increase the effort as is frequently required in distance racing.

Type 2 These are longer but manageable hills in, say, the 800m to 1000m range used in repetition running. The pace is mainly anaerobic conditioning pace, or may even be slightly faster, depending on the current level of development of the athlete. The recovery is a steady jog back to the start. Only when complete adaptation is achieved to this type of training should the recoveries be shortened. If the runs are relatively fast or the hill is a little steep then the stimulus is probably in the aerobic capacity zone.

Type 3 Short, steep inclines of around 1-in-6 gradient (17% or 10°)and about 100m long (Figure 11) can provide some very hard but effective interval training coupled with strength and specific speed work. These repetitions are run very quickly back to back. The recovery is an instant turn round and jog back down the hill before immediately starting the next run.

cannot be avoided and fast, flat stretches are hard to find, others dwell where not even one good hill, never mind a choice, might exist within a reasonable training distance. However, a little imagination can help a lot. Bridges with arched spans, ramps in multi-storey car parks, and even towns and cities when carefully explored often reveal suitable slopes.

Using hills is an excellent method for simultaneously building up strength and stamina that are truly specific to running. By varying the combinations of length, incline and distance, extra emphasis can be placed on different elements of running from sprinting to plain stamina. This work can be so varied as to be beneficial to runners in all events, but here the emphasis is on middle distance training.

The three types of hill work are summarized in the panel. Type 3 is best executed with an emphasized sprint drill style: a high knee lift and a powerful full range arm action. This is a dynamic anaerobic power session and vigorously engages many muscle groups. Building up to thirty or forty repetitions is very demanding if a fast pace is maintained throughout a long session, but it is well

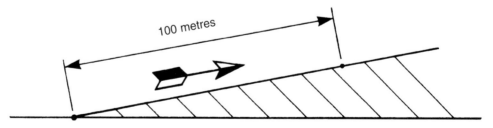

Fig 11   Repetition runs on a short, steep hill.

worth it. The stages are as follows. Progress from one set or stage to the next harder set or stage only when comfortable with the current activity. Commence the stages with each run taking, say, 20 seconds:

- Stage 1: (a) One set of ten; (b) two sets of ten, with five minutes recovery between sets; (c) three sets of ten, with five minutes recovery between sets
- Stage 2: One set of twenty
- Stage 3: (a) One set of twenty and one set of ten, with five minutes recovery between sets. (b) one set of twenty and two sets of ten, with five minutes recovery between sets
- Stage 4: One set of thirty
- Stage 5: One set of thirty and one set of ten, with five minutes recovery between sets
- Stage 6: One set of forty

The intervals themselves are short, as are the recoveries, but because it so hard and anaerobic this session builds not only dynamic running strength but it is also a powerful aid to developing speed endurance. Those using this session for the first time are advised to be careful when increasing the number of repetitions in the sets. Do so as suggested in the table and do not build up to the target of thirty to forty repetitions too quickly. It is tough on calves and Achilles tendons.

This session has an important part in the middle distance runner's training and it is worth going to a lot of trouble to find a 1-in-6 hill with a good surface. It takes a lot of application and concentration to execute these hard runs, and fast track runners should not have to worry about their footfalls. Take care, though, this is a relatively steep slope when jogged down. Do not do it too quickly, and slow the recovery to a walk back if the knees feel any effect from jarring.

Further progress is by way of a reduction in the times of the runs. Try to reduce the time of each run to 17 seconds, and throw in the odd all-out run while maintaining the overall average for the rest of the runs.

As in all interval training, if the athlete cannot significantly quicken the pace even towards the end of a set or session it is likely that the intervals are being run too quickly for the current level of fitness.

EXERCISING CAUTION

In any book on hard training there will always be sessions that are new to some readers. As with all alterations to usage or habits in training, any change must be gradually introduced and first tried gently. This way a lot of injury is avoided.

You do not wait until the start of a race to try out a new pair of shoes, they get broken in slowly and carefully. Only a fool would rush into a first-time session of plyometrics with a long hard session. Approach all new training methods with sensible caution, but without undue nervousness.

Abrupt changes always carry a high risk of creating unwanted problems, and sand hill running is one good example. First-time running up long steep hills of loose dry sand will reveal an assortment of muscles, tendons, ligaments and small joints that you never thought you possessed. The damage might be more than just the aches and pains that pass with time and massage.

When training in Switzerland with Seb Coe and Tom Byers, the all-time great Kenyan, Mike Boit, found this out much to his cost. He was the one who could not resist the challenge of a long run up a steep funicular railway track he had never seen before. The agonies of the next few days while he received remedial treatment emphasized the mistake he had made.

The very high level of intense training that is required to join the ranks of the truly elite is not achieved overnight. If interrupted by injuries the long, slow, steady progress is easily delayed and becomes unsteady.

≡10≡
RACE TACTICS AND STRATEGY

THE 800 METRES

Racing places many demands on the athlete, physical and mental. In the 800m these demands reach their highest combined intensity, which is why the event is so fascinating. Pure sprinting may be faster, but 49 second laps are very close to 400m racing and no other race demands such sustained high speed while coping with acidosis and the hazards of running in a bunched field. The 800m is very different from longer races, which call for longer concentration. The 800m calls for a very heightened level of awareness.

When racing against one's peers in top-class international competition the winner will often be the one who despite the effects of high lactate levels has stayed sharper and read the race more astutely than the rest. The heart may pound but the brain must not. All the sensory antennae must be receiving so that the runner has the maximum possible awareness of all that is happening around him.

For example modern synthetic tracks are quite silent, and in any case not much can be heard above the noise of an enthusiastic crowd, so at night quick looks at shadows on the track can be very revealing – as can the large video screens often placed over the centre of the bends. Even when the time for the first lap is called out it often cannot be heard. So, without losing concentration on the main task, try to get a quick look at the big digital clock as you pass or approach it.

Any information on who is closest in the field, the condition and positions of the rest of the opposition, and a good assessment of your own finishing potential has to be fed, unclouded, into the portable computer in your head. Accurately judging pace, correctly deciding whether to make a long run for home or timing the right moment to make the final strike are crucial to success. *Smart tactics depend on the athlete knowing what is happening all around.*

Good 400m speed may require its quota

99

The spoils of successful running. Seb Coe in Oslo in 1980 after breaking the 1000 metres World Record for the first time, with trophies from previous 800 and 1000m records.

of brute force but ignorance or stupidity is usually fatal, especially in the 800m. The lack of a good 'racing brain' is very obvious to the informed onlooker.

The Start

Each lane has advantages and disadvantages so do not worry unduly about the draw – just make sure that you know how to make the best of it. Being drawn in the outside lane prevents you from seeing how fast the back markers have started and it is very easy to find that you must accelerate too quickly trying to make up the lost ground – not the most economical way to start. Nevertheless, you do not reach the break from the lanes in the same difficult situation in which those on the inside can find themselves.

To make a good start needs good pace judgement. If you have practised it and learned to assess it accurately then you will know the right starting pace that will keep you in touch with the leaders and still be able to maintain from the lane break onwards. For the less sure the following can be a good guide. If you can sense runners on the inside, then they are gaining on you. However, this will not matter if you have chosen the correct pace for the first lap – they may be starting far too quickly.

In most races the field settles down after a very fast start. Immediately after they break from the lanes all the 'lemmings' will make a dive for the inside lane. Intent on running the longest way, they force those inside them into the heart of the pack, all jostling for a place (usual-

ly the wrong one). Meanwhile the runner in the outside lane – and any other competitor able and smart enough to resist this surge – can slowly move over in a straight line. This is the shortest route, leading to the outer edge of the inside lane at the point where the back straight joins the bend. The runner can then choose just the right time and place to join the pack without being impeded – the best position being on the white line of the inside lane, just behind and to the outer side of the leader.

From this position it is possible to cover any break, and the runner will not get trapped in the pack. By holding ground you cannot be passed on the inside; that route is blocked by the leader. If you are passed on the outside, the overtaking runner will automatically move onto the kerb – trapping the previous leader but leaving you with a clearer run. This will be your best position for the rest of the race until you strike for the home. Even if passed by a surging group you are still much safer because it is easier to move out from this position than from the kerb.

Front running is an acceptable tactic in its own right, providing an athlete is definitely faster and stronger than the rest. Otherwise, holding on to a position from which any break can be covered is essential.

There is a good reason for leaving a space in the inner lane after the start: pacemakers are often drawn on the inside. If there is one in the race he might not have managed a fast start, and if you want to exploit his or her presence it is wise to leave a gap through which the pacemaker can get to the front.

At the start those drawn in the middle lanes can see the outer runners and pull on them. This helps them to judge the pace at the start but they cannot see those in the lanes behind. This situation needs good judgement and a firm resolve. A runner now has to choose to continue at what he or she thinks is the correct pace (and after the break resolutely resist being shoved over and buried on the inside) or go to the front, get clear and then choose his or her position. Only the very best can make their way round from the back of the field and still catch up, and this is not always achieved in top-class fields.

Physiologically there is not much advantage in making a slow start. The first 15 seconds or so of the race are largely anaerobic, so it does not make sense to waste this time by going too slowly. In any case it is easier to ease up than speed up in an energy-costly effort to catch a fast moving field. Just think of the true nature of the 800m event. With the world record standing at 1:41.73 it is now an extended sprint. Catching up in sprints is always very difficult.

Alas, for those drawn in the inner lanes it can be worse. They can see all, or nearly all, the other runners but if they do not get to the front, or very close to it, at or soon after the break from lanes then they might be buried in the pack and the race may be as good as won before they can get a clear run.

To add to these difficulties races are now being promoted in which two or even three lanes will have extra runners to add to the scramble at the break. All athletes should protest against this. The use of pacemakers is another complication unless the organizers explain who they are and exactly what is their role; this is not always made clear. Beware of having a 'favoured' athlete in the race when the promotion may be a little economical with these facts.

Find out as much as you can about pacemakers, but trust your own pace judgement at a time when its accuracy will be more than crucial. Try to keep up with them, up to a point, but do not try to stay with a suicidal pace unless the best runner in the field is. This usually means that he or she is in top form and is going for a very fast time. If he is, now might be a good time to find out just how good you are.

There have been some fine races – even records – in which the second lap was much faster than the first, but of recent years the really fast times and records have had the opening lap as the faster of the two (as they were in the last two world records for this event). It is often the speed of the start while runners are still fresh that produces the faster opening lap, but once the start is over even-pace running is the more economical way to progress.

There are other reasons that make the opening lap the faster of the two. One is that the best runners are nowadays faster, better trained and can buffer acidosis better, and another is that it has become increasingly dangerous to play the waiting game. Those who try to keep it slow and trust to a short, fast finishing sprint simply do not get into major championship finals. If they do not qualify by right then they are never among the fastest losers. Heats and finals are now contested by runners who have good finishes and who are also capable of sustained speed.

Because of these latter points and all the problems that can arise in a race, I always strongly advise middle distance runners to develop fast and repeatable 400m speed. In this context repeatable means that it can be called on more than once in any race.

Mid-race

Once the field has settled down after the start the best place is running in the inside lane but close behind and slightly to the outside of the leader. This is usually done by running on the white line.

This is anathema to the dogmatic who argue for running the shortest distance at all times regardless of what it may entail, but almost certainly they will not have calculated how little the extra distance is. It does not apply when running down the straights. Running abreast of the leader requires being no more than a mere 20 inches (51cm) per bend farther out, thereby running no more than an extra 63 inches (160cm) on each curve. At 8 metres per second (50 second lap pace) this takes only 0.2 seconds. This is less than a single stride, and only a fraction of the time that can be lost trying to extricate yourself from the pack – which would be fatal on the last bend when the leader is already letting loose a finishing burst. Most

would agree that 0.2 seconds is a very small premium to pay for the added assurance of a clear run!

Not all 800m races are run by excellent and experienced fields: occasionally one or two of them will show a fault that is a hangover from the not too distant past. During the third 200m – mainly in the latter part when sensing the approaching climax – the field starts to bunch up as the runners prepare themselves for the finish. Those at the back catch up and often add to the elbowing and jostling. If the leaders had previously established any gap it is now lost, and the effort wasted. More runners are able to contest the finish.

There has always been this tendency for a slow-down in the third quarter of middle distance races as the runners try to conserve energy for the finish. But this makes it the right psychological moment to hit the rest by piling on the pace. It is very disheartening for athletes to find that just when the pace is really telling on them someone else is fit and confident enough to make it even harder! It cannot be stressed too strongly that hard, race-specific training, *learning to keep going all-out when your body is screaming for you to stop is essential to becoming a champion.*

An important part of successful racing is decision making. Some tactical decisions, such as front running, may be made before the race, certainly when experimenting or when believing that you know the best option for winning. This may even include deciding how or when to strike for the finish. This is acceptable when trying out various options but do not experiment in serious 'win or bust' situations. It is not easy or always possible to control the way the race unfolds, there being so little time in which to correct mistakes. Success will rest on staying very alert, reading the race accurately and responding instantly to any threat. The nature and the timing of the finish will depend on it.

When to Strike

There is a choice between an early strike and a late one. If you decide to make a long run for home, it may be wiser to wind up the pace slowly and steadily, or you may choose to accelerate fiercely to obtain a big, disheartening gap as soon as possible (though you risk being unable to sustain it). If the strike is a late one then it must be a killer; the timing is of the essence. It should be early enough to pre-empt any other attack and late enough to prevent any effective reply. This is easier to accomplish in a slow race but difficult in a genuinely fast one.

A 1:45 or 1:46 pace is the limit from which it is still just possible to produce a real kick, but in anything faster the winner will be the one who slows up the least. It is a race without mercy for the slow or hesitant, which is what makes the event such a test and so exciting.

It might be useful to define the word kick. Kicks come in two forms. The first is a sudden and astonishing acceleration from a good pace. In only a very few strides it takes a runner well clear of the pack. Steve Ovett first perfected it to a very high level, and he was followed equally successfully by Seb Coe. The sec-

ond – not quite so spectacular but even more deadly – is when the final nail is required in the coffin. If after mounting a serious attack the result is still in dispute, the answer is finding yet another gear over the last 80m. This was Seb Coe's contribution to the state of the art; his personal touch. It was these skills, added to a solid endurance base, that enabled him to dominate the middle distance events for so long.

THE 1500 METRES

This is the Blue Riband event of the track. It takes twice the time of the 800m and if this doubles the time during which mistakes can be made it also doubles the time available for correcting them. This puts the need for repeatable 400m speed into sharp focus: it is the key to survival. The real difference between the 800m and the 1500m lies not so much in the duration (though maybe this makes the 1500m a little harder for 400m/800m runners) but in the fact that for most of the race the 1500m is a little more forgiving of tactical error – so long as you stay alert and do not compound any errors.

Using the formula in Table 9 (in Chapter 8) an 800m run in 1:44 is worth 3:32 for 1500m. In the first the average speed is 7.69 metres per second and in the second it is 7.07 metres per second. This difference might not seem much but it is 32m per lap, which is a very long way when racing at this level. This extra pace is very telling on a runner. If it were maintained for the whole 1500m the race would finish in 3:15 – clearly an unsustainable pace for this event. Now 7.07 metres per second is not slow, and even a small increase in pace brings with it a rapid increase of acidosis. It is not easy to judge pace at speed, especially when fresh during the beginning of the race. This underlines the necessity of acquiring good pace judgement and being able to interpret the antics of some pacemakers correctly.

The Start

As the start is from a curved line drawn across the track, knowing where the other competitors are is not a problem. What is a problem – and it can happen easily and very quickly – is finding yourself in the middle of a free-for-all half way round the first bend and still locked in the pack for a long way after.

Some of the advice about the start in the 800m holds good for the 1500m. The best tactic at the start is to get out quickly, establish a good position near the front and stay in the second lane. This is the best place to be when the field enters the back straight and starts settling down. From this position it is easier to avoid getting buried in the pack. Then, after running that little bit wider, slot in just behind the leader or leaders at a time of your own choosing.

Mid-race

For the rest of the race the options are clear but not so easy to follow. One is to try to maintain an even pace as the most economical means of achieving a fast time, but you risk being too far adrift to get in a good strike. The other is to cover every break, always being close up and never being out of the second or third spot. This is more costly in energy because it will involve several accelerations to cover any changes in the leaders or any surges by them on the way round. Again, it emphasises the need to possess repeatable 400m speed and a quick change of pace. Being in the wind shadow of other runners is more significant in the longer race, the more so in windy conditions when the advantage might be as much as 20 per cent of the wind resistance.

Frequently, some runners cannot hold on to the pace and others think they can catch up later, so the field strings out. This can be fatal if those in the lead make an early strike. If this happens before those at the back are able to respond to the acceleration at the front, the leaders might be away and gone for good. Whether they are genuine front runners or athletes who have shrewdly read the race, it makes no difference. You cannot assume that they have gone off too quickly and are certain to come back to the pack. If you are surprised by a miraculous finish that has come from the far rear to overhaul the field and win, just pause for a moment to consider whether this truly reveals the quality of the winner, or reflects more on the quality of the field.

The third lap is critical. If the field is still bunched after two laps, now is the best time to get rid of those with the least speed endurance who are relying on a sprint finish. This manoeuvre seldom needs all-out speed, just a sufficient

The author with Seb Coe at Zurich on 19 August 1981. With a time of 3:48.53 Seb had just broken the 1500 metre World Record for the second time, and the look between athlete and coach says it all. For long term success there must be perfect empathy between both.

increase in pace to draw their sting. It is not always necessary to take the lead to effect this speed up. The race can often be controlled not from the front but from being on the shoulder of or just behind the leader or leaders, who sense the pressure and feel forced to step up the pace to an uncomfortable and fatiguing level.

For a fully fit and well-trained runner there is seldom any advantage in allow-ing the speed to drop in the third lap, especially in the qualifying rounds of major championships. A good pace keeps out those whose only hope is to get lucky, and if you fail to qualify because of a silly mistake (like being over-confident and easing up too much at the finish) a fast time gives you a better chance of getting through to the next round as one of the fastest losers.

The Finish

Generally the same rule applies here as in the 800m – get into the ideal position and strike from there. This is much easier said than done. Choosing how to finish is the same problem for all events above 400m, and the choices are all the variations between going early and going late. They are frequently tactical rather than strategic, often a response to the way the race unfolds. However if you are confident and good enough then it is possible to control and execute a pre-planned finish.

A big difference between 800m and 1500m racing is that in the longer event the last lap is nearly always the fastest lap of the race, even in world and Olympic records. Again this emphasises the need to couple speed to endurance, and all the previous observations on a finishing kick are very relevant.

In the final of the Moscow Olympics 1500m in 1980, Seb Coe and Jürgen Straub fought out the last lap with each successive 100m faster than the preceding one. It took a last 100m of 12.1 seconds for Seb to win the title. The opposite is true of the shorter race. The faster pace and the quicker accumulation of higher acidosis during a hard 800m ensures a slower second lap, although the split has been close in some very fast races.

Tactics

Obtaining the best position and timing for the finish depends mainly on being an alert, quick-thinking opportunist who is able to seize and successfully exploit any change in the pattern of the race. Put another way, it is better to be an adaptable, quick-reacting tactician, able to read the race as it progresses, than to rely on some master plan and trust that the race will unfold in the way you expect it to.

For instance, thinking that you know all about the other competitors and the way they run, your pre-race strategy is to wind up the pace steadily from the bell and go all-out over the last 200m. But before reaching that point you find that the lead is already being fiercely contested by two runners both determined not to yield. In this instance it might be better to let them use up their physical and mental reserves and to delay your attack until later, even until the last 80m.

Being alert is essential. In the 1982 European Championships 1500m in Athens a young Steve Cram sensed a pile-up going on behind him and smartly chose that moment to launch a winning attack before those involved could recover. Daydreaming will lose races.

Important as it is to have a sharp tactical sense it is not the be all and end all of competitive running and it must be kept in a proper perspective. Icing transforms a good cake into a very special offering, but if the cake is poor all the icing in the world will not make it a good product. The same is true for tactics and strategy. Their successful use depends on knowing your own ability and having a justified confidence in it built on *comprehensive training and a lot of good and varied experience.*

≡11≡
EVENT ANALYSIS

If an event is thought of as a chain and the basic elements of the event as the links, the performance of the chain will be limited by the weakest link. The aim of successful training is to strengthen any weak links and to maximize the athlete's performance in the long term. A short career of a year or two, no matter how meteoric, cannot be considered a success. A slow but steady progress reaches a higher and longer lasting level of achievement than any rushed, over-intense training regime.

The true nature of an event is revealed only when it is broken down into its constituent elements. Breaking it down into separate parts makes it easier for the coach to analyse a performance and pinpoint any errors or deficiencies. Looking only at the times of a performance is too simplistic – this may show that the lap splits were not right, but it will not tell you why, how and where they were wrong.

Training for the 800m and 1500m is very similar, and the differences are in emphasis rather than in content. Because the qualities for success are similar these events have a common foundation on which to build middle distance training.

Event analysis is more than identifying the physiological and psychological demands of the race, it also requires an accurate ongoing assessment of how well the competitor is doing to match these requirements. Real success in coaching is a joint achievement with the athlete, but the limit is set by the athlete's talent – so a major contribution from the coach is an early recognition and accurate assessment of its depth.

Realizing the athlete's full potential requires the elimination, or at least a large reduction, of any faults or weaknesses. The earlier they are identified the sooner they can be rectified. Success at the top demands very hard training so any mental or physical shortcoming will need building up to withstand it. No runner ever arrived on the scene as the perfect competitor with all his or her potential fully realized.

SPECIFIC TRAINING

In training be specific but be clear about when it is. The most specific training for fast running is fast running, but working on some of its constituent elements it may be quite specific although using non-running training. If weight training or plyometric training is required to produce the leg strength for high-speed running, then the correct programme that does this is also very specific at the time. It does not supply the correct style, technique or neuromuscular co-ordination of actual high-speed running, but without it there will be no high speed.

It has been proposed that the training can be based on the aerobic and anaerobic content of the event. For example, if the event has a 60/40 ratio then the training would be 60 per cent aerobic and 40 per cent anaerobic work.

This would not suit everyone. Firstly it ignores where and how the major difficulties arise in the race and what the training sessions should be to meet these demands in world-class performances. Moreover, it is not clear which ratio is the most reliable. There are significant variations between the findings in even the most serious studies, maybe because different protocols are followed or different formulae are used.

Secondly, is it an all year round ratio or only at particular times? By analysing the early but detailed diaries of Seb Coe we found that averaging a 65/35 aerobic to anaerobic ratio for the full training year gave good progress with economy, but some periods within the year were almost wholly aerobic or anaerobic to maintain a balance between speed and endurance. A better method is to treat each athlete as an experiment of one, pinpoint any deficiencies and work continuously throughout the year to eliminate them. *Give priority to those elements that will yield the greatest improvement in performance.*

The 800m and the 1000m are two closely related events in which the most limiting factor is the rapid accumulation of lactates. One approach to improving performance is to raise the anaerobic threshold by an increase in maximum oxygen uptake, which can delay the onset of acidosis. Unfortunately this wear and tear route shows rapidly diminishing returns and might not be the key to much further improvement, as all good middle distance runners will have established a good maximum oxygen uptake anyway. At 75 ml/kg/min and over there is not much point in slogging away trying to raise the figure for races lasting barely 1:45 and just over 2:00 respectively. While Seb Coe's training diaries indicated the best aerobic and anaerobic mix for him, more importantly they were a record of how much hard anaerobic speed work was done, and where it was located in the overall training.

Although there might be some variation in the estimates of the ratio for each event, they are all based on the distance being run with the athlete's best effort and not simply on the time taken. Therefore, providing the effort is maximal, each ratio should hold for a spread of times. Many a star athlete has run a fast time more easily than a lesser athlete who finished in a slower time but ran to exhaustion. In short, the effort might be much more significant than the time in determining the anaerobic content of the run.

Peter and Seb Coe. A good example of synergism: the old and the new or when two heads are better than one. Successful training is not only hard work but involves much thought and decision making.

AN EXAMPLE OF POOR ANALYSIS

The following is one good example of how failing to analyse an event correctly can lead to much frustration and disappointment. In the early 1970s there grew up the idea that 1500m runners had to be powerfully built and at least 1.8m tall, in the mould of Jim Ryan and John Walker – admittedly at that time the advocates of this theory had some good examples on which to base their faith. Although a longer historical view of the sport did not support this view, it gained ground and lent credence to a new piece of dogma.

Based on this new thinking there developed the idea that good 800m runners had to be big powerful 400m runners who had moved up a distance: sprinters who were speed and not endurance based. The harm done here was in stereotyping athletes by their physique and failing to understand that middle distance racing is very much endurance based.

This allowed the notion of 'sprinter' type superiority to spread, and one form of this idea is still around today. It is shown when athletes who feel that they are not making it at 400m, and thinking they already have the necessary speed, believe they can successfully move up a distance without the right background. This has proved to be wrong by the number of fairly good 400m runners who fail to make the grade when they make the change. You have only to watch them to see the fatigue that shows from about 550m onwards. It is even harder for the 400m/800m runners to succeed at 1500m, which calls for even more endurance – most of them are wise enough not to try.

No matter how essential it is for all middle distance runners to possess good 400m speed and a good change of pace, it must be understood that they are in events that have a significant aerobic content. It is not simply speed but speed endurance that they must have. Very fast 800m and 1500m racing should be based on the firm foundation of good cross-country and road running – best acquired when young and as soon as they start serious training. The 800m event has come a long way from the days of the fast sprinting Rudolf Harbig and a serious deficiency like a lack of real endurance training cannot be made up late in the day.

Admittedly, Seb Coe ran the least mileage he could get away with, particularly during his early years, but this was only out of prudence, and he always did just enough to achieve the relevant physical condition. But those early years were in the hard school of northern cross-country racing and some fast road racing. Although his annual total was kept as low as possible, he did have to put in several weeks of high distance 70–80 miles (110 to 130km per week) during his build-up in the years containing records and major titles.

The ultimate goal is gaining major titles, not winning one-off races. Surviving three or four hard rounds demands plenty of stamina. Think of those who ran the 800m and 1500m double in major championships and achieved medals in both, including a gold in one or other event. Seb Coe, Steve Cram, Steve Ovett, and especially Peter Snell who got two gold medals, were all distance-based athletes. If the build-up in distance is slow and steady over the early years – always with some speed work mixed in – there is no better mental and physical base from which to start.

In answering the question 'how important is tradition to winning?' Harry Wilson replied that he didn't think it much help to athletes if they were not well trained and fit enough for the job. This is also the answer to those who do not realise that moving up from 400m into the M.D. events, without an adequate endurance base, is unlikely to be blessed with success.

Physical stamina and mental toughness are needed to run six or seven hard middle distance races in eight or nine days in a major championship like the Olympic Games. A sprint background does not supply these qualities, and using only long-distance work fails to achieve the conditioning that meets the high anaerobic demands of hard 800m and 1500m racing.

ANALYSIS OF THE 800 METRES

For a better understanding of the 800m event consider a race in which the winner has a best 400m time of 48 seconds and it is run in 1:43.50, the opening lap is only 50 seconds, and to make matters worse the first 200m takes only 24 seconds. This is not exceptional; Johnny Gray raced just like this in Lausanne.

The first 200m is off a standing start and as he will not achieve his VO_2 max immediately it will be, as near as makes no difference, run all-out by our winner whose best 400m time is 48 seconds. (Although I have some reservations about the accuracy of these aerobic and anaerobic ratios, those quoted for the 200m race are around 10/90.) The anaerobic percentage will not reach 90% but it is obvious that so far he will be running substantially anaerobically and incurring a marked oxygen debt.

To complete the first lap the next 200m will take 26 seconds. This is often a settling down period when the field sorts itself out after a fast start. There could be a slight easing up but it may also be the time when a surge is needed to ensure the runner maintains the place he wants.

Totalling 50 seconds, this unevenly run first lap will average an overall 96 per cent of this runner's maximum pace for 400m. Again this will not reach another often quoted anaerobic content of 70 to 75 per cent but will certainly increase the oxygen debt and the accumulation of unmetabolized lactates. Against this background he is committed to another hard 400m.

The second and final lap is run in 53 seconds. His average pace for the next 400m will drop to 90 per cent of maximum but the effort will become so close to 100 per cent that he will struggle to continue at this pace until the finish. Having started the last lap already fatigued and forced to continue as hard as he can, for him it will be the very close equivalent of running an all-out 400m race – which has a commonly quoted 70 per cent anaerobic content, as it appears that it is the level of effort that is so important. But this assessment is made more difficult because the runner has already incurred a significant oxygen debt.

Obtaining an accurate figure for the anaerobic percentage during the second lap would require a very clever set-up, but in physiological terms the second lap is very different from the first. Providing the correct training to meet the demands of the second lap, particularly during the last 200m, is vital to success in the 800m. What is certain is that in modern world-class competition at this distance, producing a good finish in a good time after a fast second lap can be a killer.

A not uncommon alternative is that so far the race may have gone fairly smoothly, with our subject going very quickly but still just within his limit. In the second lap, through a tactical error or other runners' misjudgements, he finds himself boxed on entering the back straight.

Between 500m and 700m he has to make one or two hard surges, real changes of pace, to get free. These two efforts are completely draining and over the last 100m he is dying all the way to the finish as he just hangs on to win.

The 1000m

Seb Coe's 1981 world record run of 2:12.18 at the Bislett Games Oslo is taken as an example of the 1000m for analysis. This was achieved by running the fourth 200m in 26.23 seconds, passing the 800m mark in 1:44.56 and then trying not to die over the last 200m. The film of this record run reveals the dramatic effect of massive acidosis on end-of-race fatigue and how rapidly the slowing up progresses once it starts. The increasing inhibition on fluent leg action is clearly visible: Seb was striving to maintain stride length, cadence and knee lift while fighting numbness in his legs. Conventional tables show the 1000m to be less anaerobic than the 800m event. This I strongly doubt, if duration and intensity of effort have anything to do with it, but one thing is certain – if you are rapidly accumulating lactates you are running very anaerobically.

This 1000m race was not the best example of economical even-pace running, and the exceptionally fast fourth 200m was necessary to get the record attempt safely back on course. But not many middle distance races allow the athlete the luxury of an even pace. This example further highlights the need to learn how to cope with the sometimes dramatic effects of variations in the intensity of effort in different stages of a hard fast race.

What is clear is that the anaerobic demand on these runners is not neat and uniform, as represented by a simple ratio for the whole race. It varies a lot with changes in pace and effort. Whatever the overall aerobic and anaerobic split might be, it is built up with changing and sometimes repeated sudden demands for anaerobic power well above the mean and the *training must equip the athlete to meet these peak demands.*

The training for successful high-level middle distance racing must provide the correct physiological adaptation to cope with all these very high stresses. Simultaneously, the training and the general coaching atmosphere must also enhance the steely resolve that sees the athlete through such hard sessions and breeds race confidence.

An essential part of event analysis is an ongoing assessment of how well the athlete matches the demands of the event, so in meeting these requirements the correct training sessions have to be prescribed (and if necessary devised). Progressive performance targets must be set for selected stages of each year and each important stage of the complete career, and these details will need fine tuning as the training year progresses.

The Start

This is similar for both the 800m and 1000m – and in a fast 1500m often very close to a good 800m event. Look closely at the data in Table 11: it indicates some of the important physiological changes that

113

Description	Increase	Range
Heat production	X 100	up to 5000 Kj/hr
Breathing rate	X 4	increased from 12 to 50/min
Total expired air flow	X 30	increased from 6 to 180L/min
Blood circulation	X 6	increased from 5 to 30L/min
Skeletal muscle blood flow	X 18	increased from 1.2 to 22L/min
Heart rate	X 5	increased from 40 to 190+/min
Stroke Volume	X 2	increased from 70 to 150ml

Plus fuel mobilisation from storage sites (liver and fat).

Table 11   The physiological effects of a thorough warm-up.

must take place to prepare the body fully for hard, intense exertion. Such changes imply arriving at the start line fully warmed up in every way – maximum oxygen uptake at the ready – but of course athletes seldom do this. It is one thing to warm up enough to stretch safely, but quite another to be physiologically ready for maximum performance.

At small meetings it might be possible, but at big meetings the overall organization and the demands of television almost guarantee that the runners will be kept hanging around for the start under conditions in which a proper warm-up cannot be maintained.

Without a very thorough warm-up no athlete starts an important middle distance race ready for an instant call on an oxygen uptake of, say, 5 litres per minute. Neither is there an immediate perfusion of an adequate blood supply to all the working muscles. This is all very important, because it is a pointer to some of the training sessions needed to master the whole of these events. Learn to make fast starts and to continue running quickly from a warm-up condition no better than that allowed by a delayed start.

It is also desirable to get used before the start to the very deep breathing caused by maximum effort. During the warm-up a fairly fast burst of running for about 300m (around 40 seconds) is usually enough to avoid any breathing difficulty from this cause during the race.

The First 200m

This is almost a 200m race, complicated by a change of lanes half way. Much of the running is faster than the time suggests, because it commences with a standing start rather than a fast getaway from blocks, and involves at least one change of direction within this distance. Many runners, including some of the best, toe the starting line with their leading arm and leg on the same side. This causes them to dab the track with the leading foot before getting in a full stride, and they immediately lose ground. The better way is to stand with the leading arm and leg opposed and instantly start a full stride.

To run a good 200m it is essential to practise good bend running. Without having to practise starting from blocks, the work must include serious sessions to cover all aspects of 200m training, so that a fast opening 200m can be executed smoothly and efficiently. Besides, developing a good sprinting style is an added bonus for 400m speed and when working on a rapid change of pace. If indoor racing has any significant place in your training and racing, then learning good bend running is vital.

To be specific to middle distance training 200m running requires some thought. Sprinting draws heavily on creatine phosphate reserves. Careful management of the intervals and recoveries can cause super-compensation and enhance the normal creatine phosphate level in muscles, but this training is mainly dashes over distances up to 80m with long recoveries up to 10 minutes. Although it is better to learn technique when not fatigued, the ultimate aim is to be able to complete a fast 200m with an unimpaired ability to continue running quickly – even speeding up when needed – from an almost cold start.

After a few sessions of back to back accelerations over 80 to 100m this need is best met by additional training over the full 200m. This will increase the ability to maintain a long sprint and give the opportunity to acquire good pace judgement over this opening distance.

Furthermore, these full 200m sessions must be run with recoveries only just long enough for the athlete to maintain speed. In some sessions the recoveries so reduced as to produce a little slowing up. By becoming inured to repeated hard 200m repetitions the athlete will not be intimidated by fast starts or their effects. This type of training will therefore condition the mind as well as the body.

Done thoroughly, this form of 200m work is more time-consuming because it involves a heavier workload. It is an essential part of the training, however, because the end product is neither just a stayer nor a sprinter but both – a middle distance runner who can sprint repeatedly. It is important that middle distance coaches master the requirements of sprint training or ensure that the athlete spends some regular sessions with a good sprint squad.

The Second 200m

This starts with bend running, and the pace usually eases very slightly. In a fast race there will be little if any change in the athletes' positions at the front of the field. Generally, any changes are tactical and are usually made in the straight before the bell.

It is repeatable 400m speed that is so essential for successful middle distance running. In slower 800m races it is often used after the break from lanes, but in fast races it may not be needed until the fourth 100m or later to rectify or improve a situation. To maximize the effectiveness of these manoeuvres, the key to which is an instantaneous change of pace, specific training for simultaneously increasing speed and distance is needed. This is an essential weapon in the runner's armoury and only frequent practice will keep it sharp (the training is described in Chapter 9). Repeatable 400m speed is fine, but it is not much use if it takes too long to produce every time it is needed.

Good 400m running requires a high level of lactate tolerance, which fits in well with the needs of middle distance racing. Therefore, once good form and the desired speed have been acquired the training emphasis falls on maintaining this ability while shortening the recoveries. This constant hunt for speed is only a very necessary means to an end, which is being successful in races that are endurance events, even if relatively short. When constructing sessions of repetition running do not forget that *the end product has to be continuous high speed*.

Conventional lactate tolerance work is usually at 90 to 95 per cent of maximum speed, with up to 15 minutes rest – or 100 per cent maximum speed with full recovery – using intervals ranging from 300m to 600m. Speed endurance training also needs additional sets in which the rest periods are kept short. Therefore without losing speed, or not too much of it, the recovery times in these sets must be severely reduced. Much of Seb Coe's success came from the continual use of these training sessions – starting modestly early in the year and slowly but steadily reducing the recoveries. As Seb approached his peak, he was able to run at high speed with very short rest periods

and one particular set became his personal measure of readiness for top-class competition. With that set of six or eight 300m intervals, each in around 36 to 38 seconds with only 45 seconds recovery between the runs, we also used a similar session of four 400m runs in 51 to 52 seconds with 45 to 60 seconds rest.

Such sessions do not fit in neatly under the headings given to the various energy systems. They are hybrids created out of necessity and carefully tailored to the characteristics and current ability of the athlete. Every athlete is an experiment of one.

Because racing is continuous running all speed endurance work must lead up to it, and this can be done with sessions in which the farther the athlete runs the faster he goes, with diminishing recoveries between the runs. This training strengthens and sharpens the will and gets close to the continuous running of a race with a fast finish.

The Bell

From the bell, success in the race will depend greatly on how well the runner can cope with increasing acidosis. My good friend and colleague Dr David Martin puts it so neatly: 'Who buffers best will beat the rest.'

This ability can be developed by two types of anaerobic capacity training sessions. The first type is sets of fast repetition runs with the recovery time kept short, the length of each set ranging from 300m to 800m but with occasional sets of four 1500m runs. The second session is

Peter Coe in the familiar coaching environment of the training track.

very valuable, but harder to organize. It is the special Sunday session that we used to set up at Haringey. It not only produced a high level of acidosis, but was very good for reproducing the physical and mental stress of hard racing. This method is fully described in Chapter 6.

This hybrid session reproduces actual race conditions. Such a session is the best preparation for developing the iron will to run solo through any pain barrier – as in a record attempt or when desperately hanging on to a break made by a fully fit world-class athlete. The instances that immediately come to mind are Jürgen Straub's amazing effort in the Moscow Olympics 1500m final in 1980, so successfully held by an eventually victorious Seb Coe, and Joachim Cruz's terrific surge to create an unclosable gap in the Los Angeles 800m Olympic final in 1984, which left Seb with the silver.

In the same category are Seb's world record 1000m and his tremendous 'going away' finish to the Los Angeles 1500m final, ending in the Olympic record. These were the products of successfully combining mental and physical conditioning in training.

Once in a while a great athlete will manage to find just that little bit more when coming off the bend and into the finishing straight. Cruz did this in Los Angeles but he was only easing away. It can never be a sharp finishing kick when the pace is well under 1:45 – nearly always the victory will go to the runner who slows the least. Often what looks like the victor speeding up is the others slowing down more.

It is important to be imaginative when coaching or training. Just because you have not heard of something being done does not mean that someone else has not thought about it and achieved it. I once wrote that a very high level of speed endurance could be achieved by running 800m intervals at race pace with only 90 second recoveries. I was very surprised to see that in an I.A.A.F. review the editor Jim Alford, without talking to me or checking the facts or witnesses, stated quite positively that it could not be done, 'not even by Seb Coe'.

Such a session cannot be done by everyone but if Seb could do it there must be others who can – given the same progressive training and dedication. Not only did Seb do this, but he did it frequently, not on a track in spikes but as a continuous set on an undulating valley road in road shoes. All the times were well under 2 minutes, including some 1:46 and 1:49 runs. This session grew out of my deliberate policy over many years of trying to find out how high the tolerance to increasing acidosis could be developed. Contrast the certainty of Jim Alford's denial with that of an earlier letter to the French journal *L'Equipe*. An open-minded and informed French reader wrote that on such training Seb Coe could run 1:40 – surely a 1:41 run did not make him so very wrong!

There can of course be a fine line between boldness and folly, but in pursuit of very high and hard to achieve goals do not have a closed mind and use yesterday's methods. There is no need to be gullible, and certainly you should carefully examine new ideas and claims, but there is every need to keep an open mind and constantly search for a better way.

By the time Seb was sixteen years of age I had worked out quite accurately what he would have to do to break the 1500m world record six years later. Think big and think a long time ahead.

ANALYSIS OF THE 1500 METRES

In the early 1970s the regime of three slow laps and a short finishing sprint was forced to give way to front runners like Kipchoge Keino and Filbert Bayi, who could run very quickly all the way. Then Steve Ovett and Seb Coe arrived – they had it all and they dominated a decade of middle distance running. They could endure a fast pace and still produce a killing kick. They clearly possessed speed; and either by road and cross-country racing or victoriously surviving seven races in nine days of Olympic racing they showed they had the stamina to match. Some major 1500m races are still slow and tactical, but they no longer offer much hope to the slower runners even if they have a fast finishing sprint.

Endurance is the better base for middle distance racing and as the good 1500m runners must be able to run a good 800m, the endurance and stamina training should cover both events. Any difference is only a fairly slight one of emphasis, reflecting any bias in the athlete's physical make-up. Just as 400m runners who later decide to move up to the longer events are unlikely to succeed at the top

level, middle distance runners who ignore the need to work on their basic speed early in their career are only half trained. In neither case do they have the right conditioning to build on.

As the race is twice the duration of the 800m there can be more occasions when there is a need to use tactics. The ability to change pace rapidly when calling on repeatable 400m speed is invaluable. Although specific 400m work is a vital part of the training it is only part of it. Because these changes of pace are costly in energy they must not be wasted. Whether they are gradual or sudden depends largely on whether the choice is strategic or opportunist. A strategic pre-race decision to wind up the pace for a long run for home will require a smooth application of pressure, but an opportunist reaction to a chance to make a sudden and decisive break must be an explosive kick. Unless an athlete has all-round skills his or her choice will be limited in how quickly the break can be made.

It is not easy to compare the extra energy costs of slow or fast breaks. The greater the acceleration the larger the force required to produce it – but a slower acceleration, taking much longer to achieve its desired effect, may in the end prove to be a greater drain on resources. Races unfold rapidly and the correct decisions are more likely to be made by the runners who *stay alert and maintain concentration.*

The Start

From the standing start, straight ahead without bend running, there is an imme-

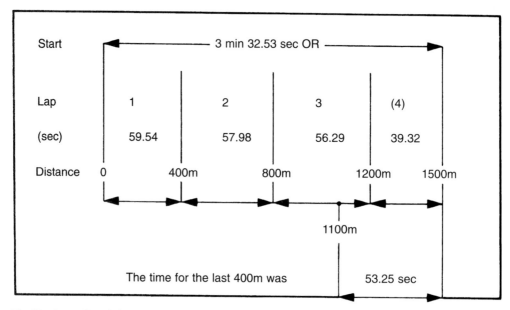

Fig 12   Lap splits of the 1984 Olympic 1500m record.

diate break from lanes. Do not hassle other competitors, but if you are caught in a scramble defend your own space very firmly.

Be sure to have a well-rehearsed strategy worked out to cope with any position you may have to take in the line-up. If a fast start is used and the runner is in a handy postition at the front he is safe for the moment and any break can be covered. If you choose a slow start, usually the result of a pre-race strategy such as saving the hard effort until the last moment, the race will get under way with you at the rear of the field.

Mid-race

After losing ground due to a deliberately slow start it might seem that the only

logical course is even-pace running. The idea would be slowly and economically to work your way to the front in time to take part in the finish. This does not work if there is a serious strike while you are still way off the pace. The only way back then is a very long burn for the finish.

Any 1500m race can be full of surprises – some become a procession for much of the race while others are all action. For about the first 1000m everything therefore depends on exercising all your skills to stay in the right place, and being alert at all times.

The Bell

From the bell onwards your alertness becomes even more critical. The sound of the bell signals great expectations on and

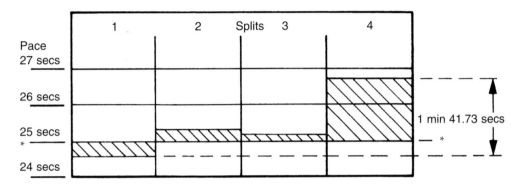

Fig 13   200m splits of the 800m world record.
* Base line to produce a time of 1min 40:0sec with even pace running.

	Split	1	2	3	4	
	Time (secs)	24.6	25.3	25.1	26.7	
Difference as a	Percentage of time	1.6	1.1	0.4	6.8	
	Change in velocity	0.13	0.09	0.03	0.54m/s	

Fig 14   Analysis of variations in time and pace of Figure 13.

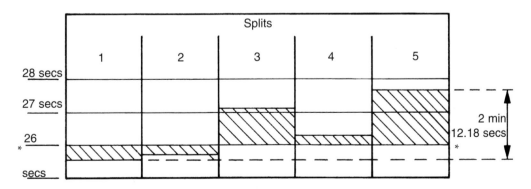

Fig 15   200m splits of the 1000m world record.
* Base line to produce a time of 2mins 10:0secs with even pace running.

121

off the track – the crowd and the athletes know that the climax is close. The pace quickens, even in fast races.

If the field is still bunched going down the back straight then some rough contacts can happen as runners try to get clear. This might call for a sharp acceleration at just the time the athletes are gathering themselves for the final sprint and it can be as unnerving and fatiguing as having to respond to a hard drive from 300m out. Again, repeatable speed is needed – but now it is for survival.

The Finish

The really strong runners like to get to the front by the end of the back straight, hold off any opposition round the curve and pull away in the home straight. Others will leave it until the last 100m or even 80m. Either way, this will be the fastest lap of the race, akin to running a hard 400m after three quick laps.

In slower races, where the advantage held by the sprinters is most marked, last lap times as fast as 50-52 seconds can happen. But that is not all. In very competitive races that are hard all the way there is no escape from punishingly fast last laps. A good example is the Los Angeles 1984 Olympic 1500m final, where Seb Coe's splits tell the story of what is still the Olympic record. They are shown in Figure 12. With each lap progressively faster than the last, which was 6.29sec faster than the opening sub – 4min lap, it focuses on the need for speed endurance. It also emphasises the value of training sessions that demand increasing speed

with increasing distance and why you should *always end a distance run with a very fast finish.*

EVEN-PACE RUNNING

Figures 13 to 15 show a comparison of the split times at 200m between the 800m and 1000m world records. The scales showing the deviations from even-pace running were selected for convenience, and tend to exaggerate any variations. While in both examples the last 200m shows the largest deviation and is obviously the slowest, one must consider the changes in speed as well as the time differences.

The obvious is all too often stated – that even-pace running is the most efficient. If it is difficult to achieve when training it is even harder with all the problems encountered when racing. Figure 13 shows that in Seb Coe's 800m world record the pace was remarkably even until the inevitable fatigue made itself felt.

The splits for the 1000m world record (Figure 14) give a similar picture. Trying to go one better than in the 800m world record by attempting to turn this event into an even longer sprint gave more time for a tactical error to happen leading to excessive acidosis. As in the 800m marked slowing occurred in the third lap and this forced a very hard speed-up in the fourth to get back on schedule.

Figure 15 is similar to Figure 13 but is based on 26 second 200m splits. The base line produces a time of 2:10 with even-pace running.

How small these differences are is bet-

122

ter illustrated when given as percentages of time (seconds) or as changes in velocity (metres per second). The variations are based on 25 second per 200m even-pace running and an overall time of 1:41.73.

Even so, the variations in 200m splits are very small, three out of five being within only a few tenths of a second, especially considering the duration of this high speed endurance. Such precision is even harder to achieve than the incredible 'metronome' lap times of the best of the African record breakers in the longer track events.

Even-pace running seldom, if ever, has a place in the cut and thrust of top-class 800m and 1500m racing.

CONCLUSION

I believe in the holistic approach to being a winner. It is a hard route, but the best one for becoming the best. Admittedly such a route is demanding but it puts the athlete's welfare first. Although I mention genetic endowment I hope it is clear that any polarizing argument of nature versus nurture is too simplistic to be useful in the pursuit of excellence and in the attempt to be the number one.

For any activity we are all born with varying capacities but this does not necessarily denote or define different abilities. Capacity is more a measure of our potential whereas ability is how well we can perform, which is most influenced by how well we have trained. We cannot exceed our capacities but we seldom reach our full potential. It is a strength of the great champions in that they are those who get closest, because they are never truly satisfied. Their eternal question is: 'Could I have done better?' The truth is, you never know – it is an itch for ever to be scratched.

Capacity can be considered as nature's endowment and ability as the measure of how hard and how successfully we trained; in short, what we have chosen to do, so to that extent it is also a measure of how we can alter some part of our environment. Choice is unavoidable, and because it is in the training equation, the permutations involving these choices and their results are too numerous to permit many certainties. If nurture includes what we do on the long hard journey to our goals then to that extent we have a substantial measure of control over what we achieve. Nature and nurture are so inextricably interwoven as to make any arguments in athletic terms academic, because there is no way of altering your genetic inheritance.

What we choose to do cannot always bring success but the wrong choices can ensure failure. In the very difficult task of achieving success at the highest level in middle distance racing it is vital that all actions are submitted to the light of reason. Gut reactions, like old myths, simply will not do. Past histories can be useful but they are not always the best guides to the future; what is needed are new and bolder concepts accompanied by searching and honest scrutiny.

Whatever your goal – good luck and make it happen!

FURTHER READING

See *Training Distance Runners* by Martin and Coe, Human Kinetics Publishers, for a more detailed background and appreciation of the application of the physiology of exercise to coaching.

Exercise and Immunology, Laurel T. Mackinnon, ISSN 1055-1325, Human Kinetics Books, ISBN 0-87322-347-0.

General Diet: *Manual of Nutrition*, Ref. Book 342, H.M.S.O., ISBN 0 11 2411146.
Success in Nutrition, Magnus Pyke, John Murray, ISBN 0 7195 3186.

Competition Diet: Diet in Sport, Wilf Paish, EP Publishing Ltd, ISBN 0 7158 06580.

A Scientific Approach to Distance Running by Dr David Costill. These books might be out of print but are good examples of dietary advice.

The British Athletics Federation has compiled a comprehensive list of sports medicine facilities. Details for your region should be available from your club or from the regional committee.

For a more detailed description of the Multi-Tier principle see *Training Distance Runners*, Martin and Coe, Human Kinetic Publishers, Leeds.

GLOSSARY

Acidosis A condition of abnormal increase in the acidity of the blood and extracellular fluids.

Adductors Muscles that draw a part of limb towards the median axis (middle).

Aerobic Depending on free oxygen.

   conditioning Endurance training done at between 55% and 75% of VO_2 max, pace.

   capacity training Around 90+% VO_2 max, e.g. interval work to produce sub-max stimuli to slow and fast twitch muscle fibres

   metabolism When the oxygen transport system supplies enough oxygen to allow the complete catabolism of carbohydrates and fat within the mitochondria of the cell.

Agonists Muscles active in generating movement.

Antagonists Muscles which can either relax or oppose (refine) the motion.

Aggression Vigorous assertive action.

Anaerobic Independant of an adequate supply of free oxygen.

   conditioning Stamina training consisting of a balanced programme of aerobic conditioning with harder and faster work.

   capacity training Fast, very intense training performed between 100% and 130% of VO_2 max pace.

   metabolism A glucose to lactic acid via pyruvate release of energy in the cytoplasm of the cell and not involving the mitochondria.

   threshold (see lactate/ventilatory threshold.)

Arousal Initiation of a response or reaction, stimulation.

Buffering Resisting changes in alkalinity or (more ususually in running) acidity.

Carbohydrates See foods

Catabolism Metabolic breakdown of complex molecules.

E.C.G Electro cardiogram, an electrically recorded graph of heart condition.

Efficiency The measure of performance cost, the ratio of input to output.

Energy systems Metabolic pathways.

   O_2 Aerobic.

   $LA-O_2$ Partially anaerobic.

   ATP-CP-LA Anaerobic.

Enzymes Complex proteins in living cells that act as catalysts. Most names ending in 'ase'.

   Co-enzymes A complex organic molecule that works with enzymes in catalysis.

Fat See food.

Ferritin Primary iron binding molecule in cells.

Food Nourishment

   Carbohydrate Simple and complex sugars. Not as energy rich as fat but a more readily available energy source.

   Fat A mixture of lipids, mainly tri-glycerides, stored as a very rich energy source.

   Protein Large complex molecules of amino acids, comprised of carbon, hydrogen, oxygen and nitrogen, often with sulphur.

   Fuel An energy source. Food after conversion to suitable form.

   Trace elements A range of inorganic elements mainly metals or metalloids in minute quantities essential for metabolism.

   Vitamins A number of organic compounds essentail for health of which there are cbout 14 major ones.

Glucose   An important sugar in carbohydrates.

Glycogen   A form of glucose occuring in muscles and liver as an energy store.

Genetic   Used as 'born with' *not* acquired.

Haptoglobin   A curculating plasma protein that captures haemaglobin released when red blood cells break up.

Innervation   Stimulation by nerve impulses.

Interval   The duration of the run *not* the recovery.

Lactate   This is produced when lactic acid disassociates into lactate ions and hydrogen ions.

Lactate/Ventilatory Threshold   The point at which after a slow and steady increase in effort the blood lactate level suddenly climbs steeply.

Lactic acid   In anaerobic energy release glucose in converted to pyruvic acid and then into lactic acid.

Metabolism   The sum of all the chemical processes that occur in the living organism.

Micro-trauma   See Trauma.

Motive   The conscious or unconscious reason for a course of action.

Motivation   The process that regulates behaviour.

Muscle   Fibrous tissue of elongated cells which contract and relax to produce movement.

Fibre types. Slow twich. Type 1. (red) activated by low level stimuli. Slower response, max, tension in 75 msec. Oxydative endurance fibres.

Fast twitch (white)   activated by high level stimuli with faster response, max. tension in 35 msec.

Type 11a   As above but with some oxydative quality.

Type 11b   Fast working fibres but also quicker to fatigue.

Myoglobin   An oxygen binding pigment, one source of redness in some meats.

Nerve   Cordlike bundle of fibres conducting information between brain or spinal cord and other parts.

Neuron   A specialised conducting nerve cell.

motor neuron   A neuron motivating muscle fibres.

Neurological recruitment   The number of additional motor neurons activated.

Plyometrics   essentially dynamic exercises specifically using pre-stretched muscles.

Specific   Meaning the most directly effective application.

Stroke/volume   Volume of blood delivered by one heart contraction.

Steroids   Hormones that enter cells and modify growth.

Trauma   Any mental or physical shocks including damage whether instant or from over-use.

Micro-trauma   Minute damage to the micro-structure as in damage to bodycell walls.

VO2 max   The max. rate at which oxygen can be removed and used from circulating blood measured as mls per kg of body weight per min.

Will   The faculty of conscious and deliberate choice.

INDEX